Fly Fishing the Tahoe Region

FLY FISHING THE TAHOE REGION

By Stephen Rider Haggard

A Comprehensive Guide to the Lake Tahoe Area and the
Truckee, Yuba, American, and Carson River Drainages

Aguabonita
Books

For information write:
Aguabonita Books
PO Box 8535
Truckee, CA 96162

Text Copyright © 2002 by Stephen Rider Haggard
Photography Copyright © 2002 by Stephen Rider Haggard
Maps by Tom Fowler, San Francisco
Maps Copyright © 2002 Aguabonita Books

ISBN 0-9652566-2-6
Printed in China through Colorcraft Ltd., HK

First Edition
M 10 9 8 7 6 5 4 3 2 1

This edition produced for Aguabonita Books by:

Barich Books
Post Office Box 475087
San Francisco, CA 94147-5087

Acknowledgments

People who write for any part of their living will tell you how much they depend on contributions from others. This is doubly true for me, since I was writing a comprehensive guide to an area so large and varied that I could never know it all intimately. The help of other fly fishers, fly-fishing guides, fly-shop owners, and of course, the California Department of Fish and Game was invaluable and freely given. My heartfelt thanks to:

Dave Lentz at the California Department of Fish and Game, to whom we all wish the greatest success in taking over from John Deinstadt at the helm of the Wild Trout Program. Eric Gerstung, coordinator of the Threatened Trout Program, and John Hiscox, district biologist at Fish and Game. Frank Pisciotta of Thy Rod and Staff Guide Service, and Jim Crouse of Alpine Fly Fishing. Ralph Cutter, author of the *Sierra Trout Guide* and owner with his wife Lisa of the California School of Fly Fishing. Jerome Yesavage, who wrote the *Desolation Wilderness Fishing Guide*. Mike Fisher, formerly of Nevada City Anglers, Bill Kiene at Kiene's Fly Shop, Gary Eblen at American River Fly Fishing. Victor Babbitt at Tahoe Fly Fishing Outfitters, Tom Brochu at Truckee's Mountain Hardware, and Andy Burk at Truckee River Outfitters. Charles Van Gelden, keen fly fisher of the Forks of the American. All the many rangers in the National Forest Service guard stations who helped me to find places and get there safely. My friends Seth Norman, writer and fly-tackle manufacturer, and Mel Krieger, who needs no introduction. Doug Matteo, who persuaded me to quit a perfectly good career to sell fly-fishing equipment—you were right, Doug. Richard Goldwach, of San Francisco's City College, who has made me a better photographer than I ever would have been without his teaching. Charles Kemper, my fishing buddy, who gets lost on dirt roads even better than I do. And last, but never least, the lovely Julie, my wife and favorite companion, who actually likes it when I bring back unusually colored rocks and pieces of driftwood.

TABLE OF CONTENTS

INTRODUCTION

Guidebooks fascinate me. I have a huge collection of them, dealing with at least twenty states and several other countries. The best of them are much more than lists of where to fish. They're authors' paeans to the rivers, streams, and lakes that they are fortunate enough to know intimately. They capture the spirit of these places, and they make you desperate to visit them.

But sometimes these guidebooks also give a hint of their authors' struggles between the desire to share all they know and the need to keep secrets. Why should we give away what we've spent so many years discovering? Is it a desire for fame or fortune? Hardly. If this book pays for gas money for future fishing trips, I'll have done better than expected. Perhaps we just have a need to tell people about the glorious, pristine places we've seen and the beautiful trout we've caught. Perhaps these places can't truly exist for us until we've told others about them. In that sense, I'm a child, dripping water on the kitchen floor, holding up a jar full of minnows saying, "Come see what I caught!"

I visited all of these waters, drove every dirt road, hiked every trail, turned over rocks to check the insect populations, and caught the trout that I found there. Many of these waters were already familiar to me, but many more were new discoveries. I visited the major rivers many times, in different seasons, and picked the brains of fishing guides and others who fish them more regularly than I. Armed with the maps I'll describe later, I scoured the mountains for any stream that might hold trout, rejecting many as marginal fisheries or too tiny to hold anything but small fry. It still left an embarrassment of riches. There are more than seventy small streams in this guide, and there is a separate listing that describes each of them, lists the trout found there, and gives directions to reach them.

There are good reasons for this bounty. Some outstanding small streams are here, of course, but good streams can be found anywhere in the Sierra Nevada. The main reason for listing them is this: When we visit the upper Sacramento River or Hat Creek on a June weekend, it can seem that we are already too many, we California fly fishers. But around nearly every corner in these mountains is a flow of cold water that feeds into the major river, forcing between mossy rocks, sustaining ferns and violets, providing a drink for shy deer and wary bears. Can you see a hook package, a soda can, a trace of human presence? No, you can't find a footprint, because no one ever fishes it.

Five Lakes Creek in the Granite Chief Wilderness.

I sold fly-fishing tackle for several years, equipping every eager beginner with a 9-foot 5-weight rod and some Humpies, Hare's Ear Nymphs, and an indicator, knowing they were probably destined to end up the same place as everyone else. After a while, I began to wonder if I might be doing them a disservice, sending them in the tracks of so many others in new waders and a half-empty vest, dooming them to certain frustration. It could be seen as the survival of the fittest on-stream I suppose— the best fly fisher wins, catches the "trophy." But just what is a trophy?

Is it an 18-inch rainbow, pulling down that yarn indicator on the lower Sacramento, one among many in that huge, artificially fertile water-delivery system? Or is it the beautiful 10-inch native that I released on the headwaters of the Downie River, or even the bear that had been watching me from the shadows beneath a tree, not forty feet away? He took off up the steep canyon walls when I stood after releasing the fish, and his precipitous rush caused a minor landslide. Then he paused to watch me again from a hundred feet above my head, with serious dark eyes and those huge black ears, straining to catch the hint of some movement on my part, making sure he wasn't followed. I'm not so stupid as to imagine he was interested in the trout I'd held, its improbably large leopard-like spots, the faint glow of deep yellow beneath the scarlet stripe on its side. But the sight of that bear made my day complete. I felt as if I'd won the lottery.

Should I have given those eager beginners a 7-foot rod for a 3-weight or 4-weight line? Yes, I think I should have. Small streams teach us everything we need to know, except perhaps the details of the insects that trout eat, and those details aren't important to small-stream trout. They can't afford the luxury of selectivity. I wanted to tell the beginners that before a trout takes a fly, that wisp of fur and feathers that we imagine to be the sole source of our success or failure, five or six other things have to happen just right. We have to find that trout, we have to not scare him doing it, we have to cast to him accurately, and not scare him doing that, either, and finally our fly has to drift to him naturally, not scaring him again. Easy, huh? Well, actually, yes it is, with the instinctive hunting ability that you probably possess and a few weeks on the casting pond. Get that fly within two feet of a small-stream trout without scaring it and you'd better believe that the fish is going to eat it.

But what about those experts among you, those who feel that your trout don't count until they get to 15 inches, dismissing them as "dinks," otherwise. Do you own a short, light rod? Have you ever tried to stop a 12-inch rainbow from wrapping itself around rocks in the tight confines of a tiny pool, or a 12-inch brown or brook trout from diving into a log-jam that's only three feet away and breaking the leader? I've tried, and I've lost as many as I've caught. I lose far more "trophy" fish in small streams than I do in big rivers, if we define a small-stream trophy as a foot long and a big-river trophy as half as long again.

But is a foot-long trout the limit of what anyone, expert or novice, can dream of catching from a small stream? I used to think it might be. Then, in 1997, I fished all season, with research for this book as my excuse, and I caught two small-stream fish of a lifetime, one a rainbow and one a brown, both 18 1/2 inches long. The length may sound suspiciously exact, but in truth, it's the distance from the end of the cork grip to the first guide wrap on my seven-foot cane rod. And that's how I measured them, laying them out along the bamboo, in awe at the size of those two extraordinary fish. And then I'll have to admit that when I got home, I reached for the tape and carefully measured the rod.

But every small stream has its pleasures, as well as its treasures, and they don't all have fins and eat flies, as I've tried to communicate. There are many streams in this book, and they're all there because I had fun. Sometimes the trout were few and far between, and any fish was a trophy. Sometimes they were everywhere, but they were tiny, and a single 10-incher was the monster from the deep. Sometimes the singular beauty of the stream's strain of trout was the thing that struck me, sometimes the vibrant vermilion of the lilies that lined its banks.

Don't try to read between the lines and find the two streams where I caught those monsters. I may not lie, but I am economical with the truth, so one of them is well disguised and one isn't even in the area covered by this book. Get out there and do your own exploring, your own searching for trophies. Choose two or three streams, fish them one weekend, then choose a different three for your next adventure. I have listed them all, every viable stream where you might hook a fish that would put a satisfying bend in a small rod. I have listed them all and made them all sound lovely because, well, they are lovely. Go and explore them, and for once, I hope we don't meet on the stream. I hope you meet no one. I didn't—just a bear, an otter, some lilies, and a lot of beautiful trout. They were all trophies.

Although I believe every viable stream is listed, if you do find some tiny gem that I've missed, by all means keep it to yourself. Is it a risk, telling everyone about what may be fragile fisheries? Perhaps, but experience suggests that the majority of California's fly fishers won't walk more than a few hundred yards from their vehicles, and of those who will, most will do so only if big trout are involved. Size does matter, it would appear. It's also true that all streams and all wild trout need friends, so the more people who know these smaller waters, the more chance that logging damage or grazing erosion may be noticed and acted upon. If we restrict our fishing to some two dozen major fisheries, treating them as "fly-fishing reserves" for our personal amusement, we can hardly complain if small streams with beautiful, possibly unique strains of wild trout aren't protected by the National Forest Service.

Note that I've said that every *viable* stream is listed. While I would encourage anyone to share in the pleasure I took in poring over maps, planning expeditions to likely streams, and exploring places where no one seems to fish, the fact is, not every small stream is a viable fishing destination. To forestall frustration and disappointment, I've also noted a few smaller streams that I've found not to be viable fisheries. That doesn't mean that they can't be fished—just that, for the reasons I give for each stream, you might spend your time more profitably elsewhere. However, I would be happy if you proved me wrong.

There are lakes listed here, as well, though by no means every lake that one might fish. I've concentrated on pleasant fly fisheries within two hours' hike from a road, particularly those that have a population of wild trout. The large man-made lakes and reservoirs, with many campgrounds, lots of planted trout, and heavy bait-fishing pressure aren't discussed. This doesn't mean they don't provide good fly fishing. Indeed, big lakes such as Hell Hole or Ice House Reservoirs probably offer the best chance of catching a truly large trout. I just don't fish them much, myself, because I don't like float tubing when the wash and noise from motor boats disturbs the lake. I can't claim complete knowledge of all, or even most of the hundred or so lakes in the Desolation Wilderness, but I will tell you how long the hike is to the ones that hold fish, and what trout can be found.

In describing the fisheries, I tried to keep my antenna tuned to the differing needs of beginners and more experienced anglers. I hoped to point the beginner toward streams that might be forgiving of a sloppy cast while providing the more experienced with new challenges in new places. I also hoped to give anglers from other states, or even other countries, an idea of the fly-fishing riches to be found close to California's greatest natural wonder, Lake Tahoe. Most of all, though, I wanted to give a sense of the beauty of the surroundings and the unique strains of wild trout. If I erred on the side of describing these things, I make no apology.

The Rivers, Lakes, and Streams of the Lake Tahoe Region

You would be hard-pressed to come up with any area of the Sierra Nevada that offered the same variety of fishing as the Lake Tahoe region. Nor could the Lake Tahoe shore streams, the lakes and streams of the Desolation Wilderness, and those of the region's four main river drainages—the Truckee, Yuba, American, and Carson Rivers, be more different from each other. To help you navigate your way through the chapters that describe this variety, here is a brief overview.

The Tahoe Shore and the Desolation Wilderness

Lake Tahoe has many lovely small streams flowing into it, but they don't open for angling until July 1. They offer varied fishing for brook trout, rainbows, and a few browns. The upper reaches of the Truckee River are now the very first fishery in the state's new Heritage Trout Program. You can catch and release wild Lahontan cutthroats in this small stream if you're prepared to hike to get there. These pretty fish are the native trout of Lake Tahoe and the Truckee River and were once almost extinct in the drainage, but the Department of Fish and Game reintroduced them above a waterfall, where they recolonized the stream better than anyone had hoped.

Above the lake to the west is the spectacular Desolation Wilderness, dotted with more than a hundred lakes with trout in them. Numerous trailheads give access, and plenty of the lakes are close enough to allow you to hike in, fish, and hike back out in one day. Permits must be obtained to stay overnight in the Desolation Wilderness.

The Truckee River

The Truckee River drains Lake Tahoe, flowing eastward into Nevada. Its open, forested canyon is a little different in character from more typical east-slope rivers such as the Carson or the Walker, which both flow through high desert country. Below Lake Tahoe, the Truckee is a fine, challenging fishery, particular downstream of the town of Truckee, where the designated Wild Trout section starts. Brown trout, some of which get truly huge, share this river about equally with wild rainbows. It's a fast-flowing river with a very stable channel, since the flow is controlled largely by the dam at Lake Tahoe, and it has a variety of hatches.

The Little Truckee drainage offers some challenging fishing in lovely surroundings as small streams run through beautiful alpine meadows or cut through V-shaped canyons to join this small river. The tailwater section, between Boca and Stampede Reservoirs, has been designated a Wild Trout stream.

The Yuba River

The three forks of the Yuba differ greatly. The North Fork is the most accessible, and perhaps the prettiest, though it sees a lot of visitors. A freestone river, it runs through a fairly wide canyon with stable banks in its higher reaches, a broad flood plain in the middle, then a tighter canyon in the lower reaches, away from any road. It has wild trout, mostly rainbows with some browns, and interesting hatches. Its drainage also provides some of the best, most varied small-stream fishing, with everything from tiny meadow streams where little brookies hide to crystal-clear canyon streams with sizable rainbows. To the north is the Gold Lakes Basin, with attractive lakes, some of which hold wild trout, and spectacular scenery.

The Middle Fork of the Yuba is without question the least accessible. In its upper reaches, Milton Reservoir is one of our best-known wild trout lakes. Below it, swimming or rock climbing may be required to get through the Middle Fork's deep canyon in places to the haunts of some big brown trout. It's a place for the truly adventurous. The South Fork is divided between a roadside stream with planted trout and a canyon with some road or trail access that offers quite prolific fishing for average-sized wild trout. There are many attractive lakes in the area, some you can drive to and many that are accessible by a short hike, particularly those in the Grouse Ridge area. Fordyce Creek is the major tributary, and a fine fishery in its own right.

THE AMERICAN RIVER

The American River drainage contains the most typical west-slope rivers. They run through spectacular, deep canyons, and their flows drop a bit low by fall. But these rivers and streams also see the least fishing pressure. They may not have the fertility of east-slope streams or tailwaters, but there are still surprisingly large rainbow trout in some of them. This is also one of the most interesting areas for students of history, because it is where gold was first discovered in California. Signs of the miners' cabins, flumes, and tailing piles are everywhere in the mountains. Lovely old mining towns provide bed-and-breakfast inns, shops, and museums.

The North Fork of the American is a designated Wild and Scenic River and runs at the bottom of one of the deepest canyons in the Sierra. Only the fittest hikers will ever fish much of it, so the fishing is superb, even if the trout aren't big. The Middle Fork is similar, but a little more fertile, and because of the dam at French Meadows, its flow is a bit more stable. It also has some fine tributaries, particularly the Rubicon River, a prolific wild-trout stream.

The South Fork is a roadside stream that gets some bait-fishing pressure for planted trout, though its upper reaches harbor wild rainbows. Its drainage contains many fine trout streams, with browns and brookies, too. It's also a good camping area, with many nice campgrounds around the reservoirs. There are natural lakes, as well, and you can access the Desolation Wilderness trails and a hundred or so lakes from here.

THE CARSON RIVER

The East Fork of the Carson is a typical east-slope river that runs through open valleys surrounded by pine forest, then through a deep canyon dotted only with juniper. The middle reaches are beside a highway and heavily planted and bait-fished, but above and below are contrasting wild-trout fisheries, with browns and rainbows. Its headwaters are closed to protect the native Lahontan cutthroats, as are those of its tributary, Silver King Creek, home of the rare Paiute cutthroat. Many fine tributaries offer wild trout, and Heenan Lake is open in the fall for catch-and-release fishing for Lahontan cutthroats.

The West Fork is a very accessible stream that runs through two beautiful big alpine meadows, then a steep little canyon. It tends to offer better fishing than the East Fork, though planted rainbows can be rather too common, as can bait anglers. It has some pretty little tributaries though, and the scenery is wonderful.

Chapter 1: How to Get There, Stay There, and Stay Safe

Much of the pleasure of planning a fishing trip is in the anticipation, in working out where to go and how to get there. That's when this guide will get most of its use. I'll give detailed, turn-by-turn instructions for how to reach each stream or lake, but to follow them easily, you'll need maps. I'll describe the maps that I use to identify likely fisheries and to figure out how to get there so you can construct your own itineraries and seek out your own special places, as well. Before you go, you'll need to know what accommodations are available, so I've provided extensive lists of both lodging and campsites. Finally, you'll need to stay safe on your journey, so I've supplied some general advice on safety.

The North Fork of the North Fork of the American River.

Maps

There are three groups of maps that you're going to find useful: a map book, national forest maps, and U.S. Geological Survey topographical maps.

You'll use the map book for finding the major routes. *The DeLorme Northern California Atlas & Gazetteer* is the one you'll want, and you should be able to find it in any bookstore. It gives an overall sense of the terrain using contour lines and by shading forests green while leaving open country white. The contour lines will help you decipher where a stream falls steeply through plunge pools or runs more sedately, while the color coding will help you to identify meadow sections. The contour lines are only at 100-meter intervals, though, so you can still run into impassably steep-sided canyons where DeLorme gives no hint of their existence.

For cross-country travel on foot, then, it's no substitute for topo maps. I don't trust the delineation of backcountry roads in the DeLorme atlas, either. Solid lines represent maintained roads, while dotted lines are unimproved roads or trails. This can mean that a well-graded road built for timber extraction isn't distinguished from a jeep trail constructed over bare rock, so for travel on backcountry roads, you'll need the national forest maps.

National forest maps are obtainable by mail or in person from the individual headquarters, but you can also order maps of California's eighteen national forests or twenty-six wilderness areas from the National Forest Service in Camino. (See the information listed below.) Call them and ask for an order form. The prices are very reasonable, and there's no charge for postage. You'll also find them on the World Wide Web at www.r5.fs.fed.us. The Toiyabe National Forest is headquartered in Nevada, but you can order that map from the Camino office, too.

These maps go to a lot more trouble to distinguish the drivability of backcountry roads. Maintained roads are indicated by double unbroken lines, and if they're paved or gravel, they're color-shaded. These are drivable in any car. The maintained dirt roads, indicated by double unbroken lines, should be drivable in any car with reasonable clearance, once they've been graded at the beginning of the season. The unimproved roads, marked with dotted lines, will vary quite a bit. If the Forest Service knows they require four-wheel drive, they're marked "4WD," but this is no guarantee that roads not marked as such don't require it. If you have any doubt about whether you can take your vehicle somewhere, either call or visit the nearest Forest Service ranger station. They would rather spend several minutes advising you beforehand than several hours rescuing you after you get stuck. Some roads are marked "OHV" and are specially set aside for off-highway vehicles. Some of them may be drivable in a four-wheel drive vehicle if the sign shows they're accessible to jeeps, but most of these tracks should be avoided. The vast majority aren't near trout streams, anyway.

The other vital information given on the national forest maps is property ownership, shown by color shading, which can save you from straying onto private property. The maps don't show contour lines, however, so it can be hard to interpret the terrain or work out what a particular section of stream is like. The answer to this is of course the topographical map, and if you intend to hike anywhere, you should get the topo map, even if you're taking a maintained trail. A new series of maps of the wilderness areas does show the contour lines, though, and they're available for the Desolation and Carson-Iceberg Wildernesses. The Forest Service also produces leaflets about camping and basic maps of hiking trails for each ranger district.

Topo maps are produced by the U.S. Geological Survey. The only size available now is the 7 1/2 minute map, which covers an area about three and a half by four and a quarter miles. The simplest way to get them is from the office in Menlo Park. Call, write, or fax for a free chart that shows the areas covered by the individual maps, then order what you need. (Again, see the information listed below.) There are a few places where you can buy topo maps over the counter, but they often cost twice as much as they do from the USGS

To Order National Forest Maps

Attn: Map Sales
USDA Forest Service
4260 Eight Mile Road
Camino, CA 95709
(530) 647-5390, Tuesday through
Saturday, 8:00 A.M. to 5:00 P.M.

NFS Ranger Stations

Eldorado National Forest
100 Forni Road
Placerville, CA 95667
(530) 622-5061

Eldorado Information Center
3070 Camino Heights Drive
Camino, CA 95709
(530) 644-6048

Georgetown Ranger District
Georgetown, CA 95634
(530) 333-4312

Pacific Ranger District
Pollock Pines, CA 95726
(530) 644-2349

Placerville Ranger District
4060 Eight Mile Road
Placerville, CA 95709
 (530) 644-2324

Tahoe National Forest and
Nevada City Ranger District
631 Coyote Street
P.O. Box 6003
Nevada City, CA 95959
(530) 265-4531

Foresthill Ranger District
22830 Foresthill Road
Foresthill, CA 95631
(530) 367-2224

Sierraville Ranger District
P.O. Box 95 Highway 89
Sierraville, CA 96126
(530) 994-3401

Truckee Ranger Station
10342 Highway 89 North
Truckee, CA 96161
(530) 587-3558

Big Bend Visitor
Information Center
49685 Hampshire Rocks Road
Soda Springs, CA 95728
(530) 426-3609

Toiyabe National Forest
1200 Franklin Way
Sparks, NV 89431
(702) 331-6444

Carson Ranger District
1536 South Carson Street
Carson City, NV 89701
(702) 882-2766
(Call here for the area this
 guide covers.)

Lake Tahoe Basin
Management Unit
870 Emerald Bay Road #1
South Lake Tahoe, CA 96150
(530) 573-2600
(This unit manages the Lake
Tahoe drainage, which includes
nearly half of the Desolation
Wilderness and parts of both
Tahoe and El Dorado National
Forests.)

To Order Topo Maps

USGS Earth Science
Information Center
345 Middlefield Road
Mail Stop 532
Menlo Park, CA 94025
In-state: 888-275-8747 or
(650) 329-4390.
Fax: (650) 329-5130

LODGING

I have tried to list all the lodgings that are available, but a few small businesses in out-of-the-way places may have been missed because they're not listed with a local chamber of commerce. There should still be plenty to choose from in every area, though. We thought long and hard about whether to try to list prices, and in the end decided against it. A business that was a little shabby, but inexpensive might be sold to someone new, be completely refurbished, and then the prices would quite properly double. A brief phone call will get you the current price. You can make a reasonable guess from the business's name. "Fred's Cabins" are likely to be rustic and inexpensive for a family, "Riverside Motel" quite reasonable for individuals and fishing buddies, "Best Western" more deluxe and a bit more expensive, and finally "Rose's Victorian Bed and Breakfast and Tea Garden" is going to be the right place to take a new girlfriend or boyfriend who needs convincing that fly fishing does not have to involve camping on bare dirt and not washing for a week. But you'll pay for the positive reinforcement.

CAMPING

Lists of Forest Service and some private campgrounds are given in the individual chapters. You can also camp wherever you find a viable site in the national forests, as long as no restriction about overnight camping is posted. This does not mean that you should carve a campsite out of a virgin meadow, or anywhere else, for that matter. Try to use established campsites as far as possible, and if you get stuck for a site, use one of those areas that have been leveled for logging trucks to turn around—you can hardly make it worse. When you choose a spot, please make it at least 100 feet from any lake or stream, however tempting it may seem to camp right next to water. This will help to protect streamside vegetation and prevent pollution.

If you intend to have a campfire outside of a developed campground, you'll need a campfire permit, which you can obtain from any Forest Service office. It's free, and it's valid for a full calendar year. Its purpose is to ensure that you understand how to build and put out a fire safely, so read the instructions carefully. From time to time, campfires will be prohibited because of fire danger, particularly around Lake Tahoe. Check to see if

Deer Lake, Gold Lakes Basin. Quite a view from this camping spot.

there are any restrictions, and if you're in doubt, don't build one. Dig latrine holes about six inches deep, well away from any water, and cover them carefully. If you take water from a lake or stream, boil it for five minutes to kill bacteria, treat it with one of the chemical water purifiers you can find at backpacking outfitters, or use one of the new carbon-filter pumps.

SAFETY

It's pretty rich for someone as accident prone as I am to lecture you about safety, but then again, anyone involved in accident prevention will tell you that an accident is an opportunity to prevent future accidents, which makes me an expert.

Wading safety is the biggest issue. When we start fishing, we worry about falling in, and whether our waders will fill with water, but the truth is that the biggest danger is in clambering around the rocks alongside the stream. The only time I ever hurt myself, I stupidly stepped onto a sloping log while wearing wet wading boots. The fall was not something I'd like to repeat, nor was the late-night trip to the emergency room. So be cautious in the water, but be extra cautious on the riverbank, too. Don't step onto smooth, sloping surfaces with wet boots, and if you wear studded wading boots, remember that they're about as effective as ice skates on dry rocks that have been smoothed by the river. If you slip and fall over in the water, on the other hand, you'll almost certainly just get wet.

Wading, of course, is still something you should do with caution. Don't wade too deep where the current is strong, and if you must wade in heavy water, always do so in such a way that your route out is downstream, with the flow. Wading staffs are a good idea in a big river, but don't let them lull you into a false sense of security. If you should find yourself off your feet, just tread water and let the river carry you until your feet can touch down, then get into the shallows and crawl out. If you wear baggy waders, there's a simple way to prevent them from filling with water. Wear a wading belt, but first wade into the slow side of a pool up to about your waist to drive the air out of the waders before you tighten the belt. (Incidentally, if your waders do fill with water, it can't drag you down, because it weighs the same as the water outside your waders, but it will make it hard to get out of the river.)

The other main concern people seem to have is with meeting bears while fishing. I don't mind running into bears, in fact I spend much of my time in the backcountry hoping to see one, but I don't expect everyone to feel that way. If you should chance to run into a bear, it's usually seen you well before you saw it and is probably busy getting away from you as fast as it can. Stand still and let it leave. In the very unlikely event that it makes a move toward you, look around to see if there are cubs present, since you don't want to get between a mother and her cubs. Then back away slowly. Never run, since doing so just might make the bear attack. If the bear keeps coming, drop your backpack or fishing vest to distract it.

The more likely problem is encounters with bears in campgrounds. Bears are great scavengers, and they're attracted by cooking smells and garbage. Never leave trash lying around your campsite, and burn food scraps in your fire, if you have one. Always lock food in your vehicle (not that this will stop the occasional, really determined bear) and certainly never leave anything edible in your tent. Toiletries, suntan lotions, and soaps may have ingredients that smell like food to bears, too, so be careful with them, as well. Bears are intelligent enough to identify food packaging, even a cooler, so throw a blanket or tarpaulin over them in your vehicle.

Finally, if you're backpacking, put your food in a bag and use two ropes to hang it between two trees, about ten feet off the ground. The Forest Service has a leaflet that illustrates how to do this.

Rattlesnakes are probably seen by fly fishers a little more than bears, not that that's saying much. However, if you ever do run into a rattler, you'll be fine as long as you see or hear it first. The rattle is just a "Get away" warning, and if you give the snake a wide berth, it'll ignore you, since you're far too big to eat. You should always remember to look where you put your feet, though, particularly if you're somewhere rattlers might be, for instance the dry rocks at the bottom of a river canyon. Rattlers are hard to see among dead leaves, and the only one that ever rattled at me was lying in a depression full of leaves on a big rock. But that's one rattler in hundreds of trips.

Chapter 2: What to Tie on and Why

I wondered whether I could write anything of use about insects until I thought about the eager beginners who might buy this book. For the more advanced fly fishers, everything might seem already to have been said by writers who have gone to the trouble of keying out the identifying characteristics of specific insects and learning their Latin names. Of course, this knowledge can make you a better fly fisher, but does the beginner really have to know Latin to catch a trout? I believe not, so what I offer here are two simple ways of understanding the insects that trout eat and of selecting an imitation that they might eat just as happily. I expect that much of this could prove useful to more expert anglers by helping them figure out hatches they haven't run into before.

Perhaps the easiest way to select an imitation is simply to select a fly that copies the aquatic insects you see, which can be done with no knowledge of the insects themselves. The other is to acquire a basic knowledge of their behavior, then put it together with empirical evidence

Little Truckee River, Perazzo Meadows. The brown trout here have time to inspect your fly closely.

you amass yourself by observation and experiment. Once you can put these two resources together, imitation by copying and imitation by reasoning from knowledge and experience, you'll find that you can select a matching artificial for any hatch. Somewhere along the line, you may find yourself spouting Latin names for some of these bugs. As long as you don't take this entomological stuff too seriously, most of your fishing buddies probably will forgive you.

IMITATION BY COPYING

You see trout breaking the water, "rising," as fly fishers call it. Some insects are floating on the surface, so you catch one. It's half an inch long, with tan wings that are folded back around its body and shaped like a tiny tent. It's a caddisfly, but you don't need to know that. It's a member of the species Glossosoma, but you certainly don't need to know that, either. You look into your box, find a fly that length, with a wing of tan elk hair folded around it—an Elk Hair Caddis. You tie it on and catch a nice trout. Why did it take the artificial fly? It looked like the natural insects, and the fish couldn't check if it was the same until it took the fly into its mouth, the only body part with which it can sample things that may be food. It looked the same because:

> **It was the same size.** This is the most important criterion. If you get this wrong, trout probably will reject your fly.
>
> **It was the same shape.** This is the next most important criterion, so you should try to get this right. Insects flutter their wings, though, and may appear a different shape to the trout when they do so. So trout often accept a fly that appears the wrong shape to you because it's still the right size. (A Humpy in the same size might have worked just as well.)
>
> **It was the same color.** This is certainly the least important criterion, and it is questionable whether it is ever vital to get this right. Whether the insect is light or dark in color may matter, though, so try to get that right. Just don't become convinced that the exact shade of orangey-creamish olive is vital. (An Elk Hair Caddis with a green body would have worked just as well as one with a tan body.)

So, examine what the trout are eating and run through the list: **size, shape, color.**

Next we need to consider where the insect is. I gave an example of a fly floating *on* the surface, but trout can eat insects that are *in* the surface film or hanging just beneath it and still break the surface in a rise. What they're eating is often the transitional stage of the insect. These insects we're discussing are aquatic, and their immature form lives in the water, but the adult hatches into the air. During a hatch, while floating in the surface film, the adult will be pulling itself out of the skin that it had as an immature "nymph" or "pupa." We call it an "emerger."

One way of trying to interpret the trout's activity is to look at the rise form, the disturbance that the trout has just left, and see if it leaves a bubble. This clue means the trout probably took something from on top of the surface, because it also took in air that was released as this bubble. If there's no bubble, then it probably took something from beneath the surface. I prefer to put my eyes as close to the water as I can and look across the surface as a floating insect approaches a trout. If the insect floats by untouched, or the trout rises at something I could not see, or both, I reckon the fish is eating emergers. Then you can use an aquarium net or a special insect-catching screen that you can buy at a fly shop to find out what those emergers look like. If you don't think you have a good imitation, take scissors or nippers to a dry fly until it resembles the emerger, or find an unweighted nymph and grease it well with dry-fly floatant.

Finally, there are the times when trout eat immature forms of the insects, nymphs or pupae, drifting deep in the water column. When they do, they never disturb the surface at all. You don't see rising trout, but you may see the shapes of fish moving from side to side, or the white of a trout's mouth as it opens to take something. You can use one of those screens or a kitchen strainer to find out what they're eating then.

IMITATION BY REASONING

If in addition to learning to copy an insect that you find the trout eating, you learn how to identify which of the five main groups of aquatic insects it belongs to, you will know how and when it hatches and will be able to figure out what the trout will be eating at other stages of the hatch. If you can just remember a few key facts about these insects, it will help you to understand rationally what you've simply been looking at and copying, and help you anticipate what will happen, instead of merely reacting to it when it does.

MAYFLIES

These are the insects that started the whole process of fly fishing. The name is illogical, because it refers to a single, large, cream-colored species that hatches in British rivers (and lakes) in May. It's the most famous hatch in Britain, and somehow its name got transferred to the whole family in America. The more logical name, which is hardly ever used, is "Dayfly," because the adult insects live for only a day, or at least a twenty-four-hour period. The adults have no mouthparts, either, so they can't eat, nor, more importantly, can they drink water. This is a key piece of information, because it explains why mayflies hatch only in the morning or evening on hot, sunny days in midsummer. If they hatched at midday, they would dry out and die before they could mate. You'll notice that mayflies almost always hatch more prolifically on cloudy days, and now you know why.

They have a life cycle that goes like this: An egg hatches into a nymph, the immature form of the mayfly. The nymph lives underwater, discarding its skin several times as it grows. When it's ready (usually after a full year), it either rises or swims to the surface to hatch. It may take a while to get out of its skin, or shuck, at the surface, then it drifts on the water for some distance while it dries out its wings enough to be able to fly. In the spring and fall, most mayflies hatch in the middle of the day because they need the midday warmth to dry out their wings. Now you know why they hatch at different times of the day according to the time of year.

The adult insect, which is called a "dun," takes off and flies to streamside vegetation. Within a few hours, it molts once again to become the fully mature insect, called a "spinner." Mayfly duns look like miniature sailboats drifting on the surface, because they hold their wings upright, at right angles to their bodies. Their delicate wings will be some shade of gray, but fairly opaque, so you should be able to spot them. When they take off, they usually fly in straight lines, upward and away from the river. They have long tails that are held downward, so they look like tiny crucifixes moving steadily through the air. The other main aquatic insects fly more erratically, so if it moves in a steady, straight line, it's probably a mayfly.

Spinners look very like duns in size and shape, but the body color is usually different, often being brighter, while their wings are nearly always clear, rather than gray. Spinners may be found clinging to the leaves of bankside vegetation, but the males can easily be seen dancing in clouds above the trees. The female will fly into this cloud to select a mate. Mating takes place in the air, then the female flies to the water and either dips her abdomen onto the surface or walks down a stick or a rock to lay her eggs beneath the water, trapping a bubble of air between her wings as she goes. If you're standing in the river, she'll use your waders, so now you know why you find whitish patches on your neoprenes the size of a capital "O."

We call the collection of egg-laying and spent spinners on the water a "spinner fall," and mayflies at this stage of their life cycle can be hard to spot. The spent spinners will be floating flat in the film with their wings outstretched, as if they were a bird in flight, which makes them tricky to see at any distance. Look at a part of the river that flows close the bank on your side to see if spinners are on the water. Now you know the most likely reason why trout may be rising when you can't see any insects fluttering on the surface in the evening.

CADDISFLIES

These insects look like small moths. Their wings are nearly always opaque, and covered with tiny hairs. They fold them back around their chunky body when they're at rest, so they look like a small tent. Their flight is erratic, like the flight of moths, too, so they're easy to tell from mayflies. They're often seen fluttering under the bushes next to a stream or lake, or behind rocks in a river. They live for several days, even weeks, because they have mouthparts and can drink water. Now you know why artificial caddisflies are good general imitations, because caddises are frequently fluttering around above the trout, and they have to touch the water to drink.

Caddisflies have a life cycle that goes like this: An egg hatches into a larva, which lives under the water until it's almost ready to hatch, when it turns into a pupa, just like a butterfly or moth. The pupa either swims or rises to the surface to hatch. It usually takes a while to get out of its shuck, but once out, most caddises take off almost immediately. This is why an emerger pattern is often much more successful than a dry fly during caddis hatches.

Many caddis pupae swim actively to the surface, and because they represent a good-sized meal, the trout will chase them. This causes slashing, swirling rises, because caddis pupae can move faster than most other items of a trout's food. Sometimes trout leap clean out of the water because they've allowed their momentum to carry them out, having captured a pupa beneath the surface. Now you know why trout were jumping out of the water, but wouldn't take any dry fly. This is also the main reason why swinging a soft-hackle pattern, or a Bird's Nest, is successful.

Caddis hatches can happen at any time of day, but the late evening and on into dark is the most likely time to see one. This is probably an evolutionary trait that enables them to avoid being captured by birds. Egg-laying activity, on the other hand, often happens in daylight. Unlike mayflies, caddisflies don't always do this all at once, so a few caddises will be seen throughout the day, fluttering above the river and dipping their abdomens to shake off their eggs. However, one thing caddises do share with mayflies is that some species climb or swim actively beneath the water to lay their eggs, again carrying a bubble. This is another reason why swung wet flies work.

STONEFLIES

These are the most primitive of all aquatic insects. Their life cycle consists only of egg, nymph, and adult stages. The nymphs live in the very fastest water, shedding their skins frequently as they grow, then crawl out of the water to hatch. The dried-out husks that you find on the back of river rocks are the cases of stonefly nymphs.

Adult stoneflies crawl around on rocks, trees, and bushes next to the river and mate on land. They have flat wings, which they fold back along the top of their bodies so that they look like very elongated beetles. All stoneflies are slow, ponderous fliers, particularly the larger ones. Their weight makes them vulnerable to falling into the river, and it also renders the females incapable of escaping from the surface after egg laying. The sheer size of the large stoneflies makes them very desirable to trout, so stonefly dry flies are good searching patterns when the adults are climbing around.

Stoneflies mostly come in large and small sizes. Medium-sized stoneflies, from size 10 to 14, are present in only a few rivers in any numbers, but you will find them in the Truckee, for example, where they're an important hatch. The most common small stoneflies are bright yellow or yellowish-green in color, and because they fly fairly straight, they're the only insects that could be confused with mayflies. Their bodies are a little chunkier, though, and the tails much shorter, so they look denser than the more delicate mayflies. They're important to the trout when they lay their eggs, on early summer evenings.

Midges

The nonbiting midges can be the most abundant insects in lakes, even in many rivers, and they're usually the tiniest, as well. They have flat wings folded back over slender bodies. With their long legs, they look like mosquitoes, but without the biting proboscis. They have a complete life cycle, with egg, larva, pupa, and adult stages. They're most frequently available to the trout when the pupae, which look like a tiny letter "J," rise to the surface to hatch. They often do this in huge numbers, but they can be so tiny that the fly fisher doesn't notice them taking off from the water. If you see fish rising on a river and you can neither see a hatch nor find any mayfly spinners, then you should suspect the fish are feeding on midge pupae.

I've stressed how tiny most midges are, but some lakes have large midges, larger than most people have observed. This is particularly true of reservoirs and other impoundments, because evaporation tends to concentrate water-soluble nutrients brought in by their feeder streams, so these waters tend to get very fertile. Large midges can take a lot of time to penetrate the surface film of a lake in order to hatch. Trout feeding on these, or indeed on midge pupae of any size, will often swim in straight lines, rising with an economical head-and-tail motion, showing the tips of their tails as they go down. The trout can use this slow-motion method of feeding because midge pupae stuck in the surface film can't escape. If you see this kind of rise on a lake, think of midges.

Damselflies and Dragonflies

Although you can find the immature form of both of these insects in slower rivers, they're almost exclusively lake-dwelling. You'll see the adults flying in the margins of most lakes. Damselflies have long, very slender bodies, with slightly shorter wings, folded back above when at rest. Dragonflies have fatter bodies and hold their wings at right angles. The life cycle is simply egg, nymph, and adult. To hatch, both nymphs swim to the lake's margins, then crawl up rushes or reeds, where the adults pull themselves out of their shucks. Damselfly nymphs hatch in large numbers, and they swim close to the surface, so if you see swirling rises, look for these slender nymphs. They wriggle their bodies from side to side as they swim, so they look a bit like tiny water snakes.

These insects fly over the surface of lakes, both to hunt the small midges they prey on and to lay their eggs, and trout occasionally will try to grab them. If you see explosive rises or fish leaping clean out of the water in the middle of a sunny day, watch for damsels or dragons flying a few inches above the surface.

TERRESTRIAL INSECTS

Land-born insects often end up in the water. Some that can't fly, like worker ants, just fall in. Some that can fly end up in the water by accident. A very few are actually there on purpose to lay their eggs (for example, some moths have a partially aquatic life cycle). But all of these reasons are dwarfed by the significance of the wind. Regular gusts of wind will blow insects out of the trees, but on high mountain lakes there is a phenomenon called "up-slope blow in." This means that the wind blows like heck every afternoon and deposits all sorts of terrestrial insects onto mountain lakes. For high-country trout, it's often their major source of food. Look in the margins on the downwind shore to find out what's blowing in and select as good a copy as you have.

On meadow streams, or any section of a stream that has grassy banks, ants, beetles, and grasshoppers are a major food source. When nothing is hatching, I always try one of those three terrestrial patterns. If you see trout rising sporadically, close to the bank of a meadow stream, it's most likely that they're eating terrestrials.

FORAGE FISH

Big fish eat little fish. It's the way of the watery world, and trout are no exception. In Sierra streams, by far the most common forage fish is the sculpin, a dark-colored, mottled little fish that keeps itself glued to the bottom. The Truckee River is full of sculpins, and the brown trout particularly relish them. Some lakes contain small chubs or shiner minnows that I've yet to identify to the species level, but the trout don't care, they eat them and their imitations just the same.

CRAYFISH AND SCUDS

Both of these animals are crustaceans, though one is a lot bigger than the other. Crayfish are abundant in many Sierra waters, and their appearance should be familiar to most readers. They grow to as long as six inches and spend the daylight hours hiding in crevices in the rocks, coming out at dusk to feed. Trout eat crayfish when they can catch them, though all except the real lunkers apparently stick to eating the smaller ones, those less than two inches long. I've found scuds in only one or two small streams in the Sierra, but they are present in quite a few fertile lakes. Olive-gray in color and from an eighth to a quarter of an inch long, they look something like a tiny shrimp with a very short head. They're very rich in protein, so their presence is a good indicator that big trout live in the lake or stream where you find them.

MORE ABOUT HATCHES

After all of this information, you may be eager to learn more about aquatic insects. If you are, then by all means buy any of the excellent books that I've listed below. You may even start to collect adult insects or nymphs so that you can study and imitate them. It's a wonderful way to deepen your appreciation of what's happening on the trout stream. But if it all seems a little too bewildering, or you know you don't have the time to do this and go fishing, well, just remember the principles of imitation by copying: *size, shape,* and *color.*

Even seasoned angling entomologists can find identifying aquatic insects bewildering these days, though. Entomology itself has undergone radical changes in the recent past and may undergo even more in the future. The Latin names for insects that many anglers learned by reading works such as *The Complete Book of Western Hatches,* by Rick Hafele and Dave Hughes, which was first published in 1981, may no longer be correct because entomologists, now armed with the tool of DNA analysis, are able to prove definitively which insects belong in which family or genus, rather than making an educated guess on the basis of physical characteristics seen through a microscope. For instance Green Drakes, which used to be in the genus *Ephemerella*, are now in the genus *Drunella*, and the Creamy-Orange Dun, another important California hatch, is now *Seratella tibialis,* rather than *Ephemerella tibialis.* This stuff can drive fly fishers crazy, so where we know that a change in the Latin name has occurred comparatively recently, we've given both names in the hatch charts.

In what follows, you'll find hatch charts given for three of the major rivers, the Truckee, the North Fork of the Yuba and the East Fork of the Carson. The other forks of the Yuba and the larger rivers in the American River drainage will have hatches very similar to those on the North Fork of the Yuba, while the hatches on the West Fork of the Carson are similar enough to those on the East Fork that one hatch chart can cover both. You may notice that the caddisflies are referred to by the English term "sedge." I'm not trying to impose my English heritage on you. The identification of specific caddis species by fly fishers is so recent that American common names don't exist yet. These are the names that you'll find in the detailed hatch guides written by acknowledged experts like Ralph Cutter, Dave Hughes, and Gary LaFontaine.

Hatch matching is less important on smaller streams, because the hatches are seldom abundant enough to make the trout selective, but where specific types of insect are plentiful, you'll find a note in the text. The hatches of lakes are harder to study and tabulate, but the observations that I've made and the knowledge that others have kindly shared with me are both given where possible.

Some Suggested Hatch Guides

Dave Hughes. *The Western Streamside Guide.* Portland, OR: Frank Amato Publications, 1998. A good basic hatch book for the beginner in convenient vest-pocket size.

Rick Hafele and Dave Hughes. *The Complete Book of Western Hatches.* Portland, OR Frank Amato Publications, 1981. A comprehensive treatment of the subject.

Jim Schollmeyer. *Hatch Guide for Western Streams.* Portland, OR Frank Amato Publications, 1997. A new and comprehensive guide in convenient vest-pocket size.

Ralph Cutter. *Sierra Trout Guide.* Portland, OR Frank Amato Publications, 1991. Contains an excellent chapter on trout foods and a detailed hatch chart for the Truckee River.

Gary LaFontaine. *Caddisflies.* Helena, MT: Greycliff Press, 1981. The bible on the subject of these important trout stream insects.

Malcolm Knopp and Robert Cormier. *Mayflies.* Helena, MT: Greycliff Press, 1997. The definitive reference.

Pleasant Valley Creek, Carson River drainage. If you've paid to fish, you'll need the right pattern.

FLIES

I thought I might spare you the obligatory list of enough flies to stock a fly shop, not least because the five or six other things that have to happen just right before a trout ever takes a fly are more important than the fly itself. Then I thought of beginners again, so I went through my fly boxes and figured out the few flies that I actually use, hoping against hope that I might prevent those novices from acquiring the many hundreds of flies in my boxes that have never even gotten wet.

If you're figuring out what you need in the Sierra, start with the list of general dry flies and basic nymphs, and collect other flies listed here when you find you need them.

GENERAL DRY FLIES

Adams, size 14 to 20

The most useful dry fly anywhere, any time. A good imitation of dark mayflies, fluttering caddisflies, or dark stoneflies. In the smallest size, it imitates midges. If you tie your own and prefer an upright and divided wing to "parachute" styles, don't bother putting wings on the size 20s—the trout don't seem to mind.

Elk Hair Caddis, size 12 to 18

A very close second as a general pattern, and easier to see on fast water. Ironically, it can be less useful during actual caddis hatches, when an emerger may be better. I don't believe that the color matters much.

Humpy, in yellow or olive, size 12 to 16

The classic fly for broken water, easy to see and hard to sink. Particularly useful in the early season and in pocket water.

Trude, size 14 to 16

I used to think this was a dumb fly. I don't kill many trout, but I noticed the few I did kill always contained some black terrestrial insects. So I tied some all-black Humpies with black and grizzly hackle. I frequently "invent" unsuccessful patterns, but this one was spectacular in its uselessness. The more it failed, the more I used it. After seven or eight trips without a rise, I tied on a Trude, which rose every trout in the stream. This is a good example of what I mean by amassing empirical evidence through observation and experiment. Through observation and experiment, I learned that I should have listened to all the great fly fishers who have recommended a Trude. A good alternative as an attractor would be the fairly similar Royal Stimulator.

Basic Nymphs

Bird's Nest, tan or brownish olive, size 10 to 16

Not only the most useful nymph, but it can be used as a wet fly, too, allowed to swing around in the current so that you actually feel the take, which is much more fun than fishing with a bobber and calling it a strike indicator. A Hare's Ear Nymph in the same sizes is an acceptable alternative.

Prince Nymph (some with bead heads), size 10 to 16

I modify this pattern somewhat, which bearing in mind my track record (see the Trude listing), probably makes it less effective. Use the standard Prince as a nymph or wet fly.

Pheasant Tail Nymph, size 16 to 18

A close imitation of many mayfly nymphs, good for fussy trout and spring creeks.

Black Woolly Bugger, size 6 or 8

The basic streamer pattern, which everyone should have, but also a passable stonefly nymph imitation when drifted through pocket water.

Specific Dry Flies and Emergers

Sparkle Dun, olive, size 10 and size 14 to 20

Imitates a dark mayfly adult pulling out of its shuck. The largest imitates the Green Drake mayfly.

Sparkle Dun, yellow or cream, size 16 to 18

Imitates pale mayflies.

Rusty Spinner, size 16 to 20

Imitates the egg-laying female mayfly. You can get by with the size 20 if you run into a fall of the tiny Trico spinners, although these are usually imitated by flies with black bodies.

Mayfly Emerger, brown, olive, or some color in between, size 14 to 18
Some CDC (cul de canard), foam, or deer hair should be tied in to help this fly float.

Emergent Sparkle Pupa, tan and green, or some color between green and olive, size 14 to 16
These deer-hair-winged flies are the best surface patterns to use during a caddis hatch. I also fish a weighted version with a wing as a wet fly, on the swing. The Deep Sparkle Pupa, however, will work just as well.

Gold Stimulator, size 8
To imitate Golden Stoneflies and bring up larger fish. Can be used to imitate the big, orange-bodied October Caddis, too.

Little Yellow Stone, size 14 to 16
These little stoneflies can be very important in the early summer. When they are, a Light Cahill dry fly can be just as effective as this precise imitation.

Black Ant, size 14 to 16
Trout eat ants. What more do you need to know?

Hopper, size 10
Fly shops stock a range of grasshopper patterns, and the exact one probably doesn't matter, but I try to buy the ones with rubber legs. I find I need only this one size for the Sierra.

More Nymphs, Wet Flies, and Streamers

Golden Stone Nymph, size 8
Stonefly adults are available to the trout for only a few weeks, but the nymphs have a life cycle of two or three years, so they're around all season long.

Midge Pupa, black or dark olive, size 20

There are many times when fish in streams feed selectively on midge pupae drifting in the flow. This is much more common than you might imagine, and the only way to catch fish then is with this tiny fly fished dead drift. Very useful on high lakes, too.

Soft Hackle, yellow and/or green, size 14, Pheasant Tail Soft Hackle, size 16

Wet-fly fishing is quite simply the most neglected method in all of fly fishing. It doesn't always work as well as a dead-drifted nymph, but sometimes it works better, and it's always more fun. Beginners should learn how to fish these effective flies.

Lake Flies

Damselfly Nymph, olive, size 8

Bird's Nest, olive, size 12 to 16

A good imitation of the nymphs of *Callibaetis,* the most common mayfly in lakes. The smallest size listed here also serves as a perfectly good scud imitation, probably better than the "exact" copies you can buy.

Dark Feather-Wing Caddis, size 12 to 16

Most, though not all, lake-dwelling caddises have darker wings, and this more exact imitation is also useful on spring creeks in the smaller sizes.

Red Ant, size 16

Red ants (which I think are actually termites) seem to get blown onto lakes at least as much as black ones, particularly where pine trees surround the lake.

Olive Woolly Bugger, size 6 or 8
Olive Zonker, size 4 or 6

These streamers give you enough choice for most lakes. I confess that I don't fish streamers as much as I should. I'm just too eager to find and identify the insects the trout may be eating so that I can catch them at the surface. But the truth is that big trout are seldom anywhere near the surface, and a sinking line and a pattern like the Zonker is often the best way to catch a real lunker. Olive and black Woolly Buggers (the black one already has been listed as a river fly) round out a reasonable streamer selection. The olive Woolly Bugger is the best crayfish imitation, since it imitates its action better than more precise copies.

Midge Pupa and Emerger, reddish orange and olive, size 14 to 16

You need these last two flies for only a few fertile east-slope lakes, such as Martis, Heenan, and Indian Creek Reservoirs.

This may seem like a lot, but even if you were to get them all, it's just 27 different patterns, many in just one size.

Fly Fishing the Tahoe Area

A Brief Explanation of the Listings

Here is the header from a typical listing in this guide: The first three lines help you to find the stream. The DeLorme page numbers and grid references refer to the *Northern California Atlas & Gazetteer*. Single references are given for lakes, while for streams, the first reference pinpoints the headwaters, and the second marks either the mouth, or in the case of a main river, the end of the section discussed in the listing. Where the point being described is intermediate between two grid marks, both will be listed, separated by a slash mark thus: p. 70, A/B3. The national forest map is listed next, and the U.S. Geological Survey topo maps are given last.

THE NORTH FORK OF THE YUBA RIVER
DeLorme: p. 70, D3; p. 69, D6
USFS: Tahoe National Forest
USGS: Haypress Valley, Sierra City, Downieville, Goodyears Bar
Altitude: 7000–2200 feet
Water types: From beaver ponds through small pools, runs, and pocket water to large pools and riffles.
Trout: Rainbows, 9–17 inches; browns, 9–24 inches; brook trout, 7–10 inches in the headwaters.
Special Regulations: From the western boundary of Sierra City to Ladies Canyon Creek, two trout, minimum size 10 inches, only artificial lures with barbless hooks permitted.

The next line gives the altitude at which the fishable reaches of a stream start and finish, rounded to the nearest hundred feet. This can help you determine whether the snowmelt has finished in early spring, or in a lake listing if ice-out has come, by comparing it with other streams or lakes you may have fished at a similar elevation.

The listing of water types is self-explanatory and is a fair guide to what you'll find. I have used three distinct terms to describe the size of smaller streams, intending that they should not be seen as interchangeable. In descending order of size they are: small, little, and tiny.

Trout species are given from personal experience, backed up by information from The California Department of Fish and Game and from guides familiar with the rivers. The species are listed in order of abundance, starting with the most numerous. The sizes listed for each species are just rough indications of the range of trout you might catch, although any stream or river can produce the very occasional much bigger fish. Trout size also will vary with cycles of drought, since growth rates slow down during a prolonged drought. In streams, the trout can be assumed to be wild, but if any trout are planted, it will be mentioned in the text. For lakes, I have listed whether trout are planted or wild, but I haven't given trout sizes because they fluctuate even more and will often depend on Department of Fish and Game management decisions about what species and size to plant. A general idea usually will be given in the text.

Last in the listing come special regulations, if there are any. I have tried to anticipate a few forthcoming changes, but you should remember that these regulations change frequently enough that such information cannot be guaranteed to be current. You may think that if you never kill trout, it won't matter, but even then, streams and lakes are occasionally closed to all fishing to protect scarce populations of native trout. You always should check the latest regulations in a current Department of Fish and Game California Sport Fishing Regulations booklet before a trip. Pick one up where you bought your fishing license or download a copy at http://www.dfg.ca.gov/regs.html.

Chapter 3: The Tahoe Shore Streams

Lake Tahoe is a natural wonder, a shimmering turquoise enigma. When you stand on its California shore and gaze across to the distant, misty-blue peaks in Nevada, you can easily believe that you're looking at an ocean. Its sheer scale gives the lake a fantasy feel, as if your mind conjured it in the moment between dreaming and waking. Twenty-two miles in length and 12 miles in width, with a maximum depth of 1645 feet, its deepest spot is actually 92 feet below Carson City, Nevada, in the flatlands below. If it were drained to flood California, it would cover the entire state to a depth of 14 inches. Only when you climb the trails into the Desolation Wilderness can you get any perspective and realize this is just the biggest, bluest lake you've ever seen. Is it any wonder that Lake Tahoe inspires reverence in visitor and resident alike? Now, if only the fly fishing in the big lake was really good!

Upper Truckee River, below Dardanelles Lake. Brook trout are everywhere, and you'll find native cutthroats upstream.

The only native trout in Lake Tahoe was the Lahontan cutthroat. In the last century, tens of thousands of these fish, which could weigh as much as forty pounds, spawned in its larger tributaries and its outlet into the Truckee River. They were netted or trapped on their spawning runs, and canneries operated into the 1920s, sending tons of fish to the mining camps of the Sierra or the growing city of San Francisco. That was enough to threaten their survival, but clear-cutting of timber along the tributaries, together with massive die-offs in the late 1920s, wiped them out entirely by 1930. The cause was never formally identified, but was thought to be the introduction of pathogens via planted, nonnative trout.

A separate population of Lahontan cutthroats existed in Nevada's Pyramid Lake and spawned in the lower Truckee. They were rendered extinct by the reviled Bureau of Reclamation and their first, and most ill-considered project, Derby Diversion Dam on the Truckee. Luckily, some pure-strain Lahontans survived in a few streams and in Independence Lake. They were reintroduced into Pyramid Lake, and today, they're propagated by the Paiute Indian tribe. Lahontans that the California Department of Fish and Game maintain in Heenan Lake have provided fry to reintroduce into the upper East Carson River and many smaller streams. One of the most successful reintroductions has been the most recent, into the Upper Truckee, which flows into the lake at South Lake Tahoe.

Today, Lake Tahoe contains rainbow and brown trout and kokanee salmon. Lake trout, though, have been the most successful of the introduced sportfish. Like the brook trout, the lake trout is actually a char, adapted to living in the frigid depths of large lakes. Because of Tahoe's huge size and its relatively infertile water, there is really no viable fishery for the true trout, at least not with a fly. Most of the fishing done here is for the lake trout, from boats with heavy trolling tackle. The major tributaries and the lakes that they drain provide the best opportunities for the visiting fly fisher. To protect spawning runs, no fishing is allowed below the first lake on any Tahoe tributary until July 1, and the season closes on September 30. The lakes, however, can be visited as soon as the ice melts and until the snow flies in the fall.

THE UPPER TRUCKEE RIVER
DeLorme: p. 89, C7–A7
USFS: Eldorado National Forest
USGS: Caples Lake, Echo Lake
Altitude: 8600–6200 feet
Water types: Small pools and runs.
Trout: Brook trout, 7–12 inches; rainbows, 7–10 inches, larger near
Lake Tahoe; Lahontan cutthroats, 7–10 inches in the headwaters.
Special Regulations: Open for angling from July 1 to September 30.
Above Showers Creek, catch-and-release with barbless hooks only.

If you're prepared to put on hiking boots and walk a ways, you can have
one of the best experiences in fly fishing here: catching and releasing a
threatened species of trout that's bounced back from the very edge of oblivion. You can cradle a pretty little 10-inch fish in your hands and dream
of the potential recovery of the largest trout that ever lived, the native
Lahontan cutthroats of Lake Tahoe. These lovely fish have golden-
olive sides suffused with lilac, large, widely scattered spots, and a distinctive
orange slash on the jaw. They were reintroduced here, after chemical treatment to remove the nonntaive trout, above a natural barrier at the junction with Showers Creek, and that part of the stream was closed to all fishing. By 1997, they were thriving in their native environment, and they'd
even spread below the closure site. Then in, 1998, the stream reopened
above Showers Creek under the special regulations noted above. The brook
trout somehow reappeared in this stretch in 1995 under rather suspicious
circumstances, right by a trail crossing. The Department of Fish and Game
has to electrofish the brookies out every year and seem to be winning the
battle at last. The electrofishing team didn't turn up any young-of-the-
year brookies in 1999, so it appears that they didn't succeed in spawning
the previous fall.

The lower reaches of this little river could be fished in a few places
where it runs through public land in South Lake Tahoe, but I'm not keen
on fishing in a suburban setting. Like all Tahoe tributaries, the stream does-
n't open until July 1, so it gets hammered hard over the holiday weekend.
Large trout, mostly rainbows, run up these streams to spawn and stay
around to feed. Bait fishing is allowed, so many of the spawners get
killed, a senseless slaughter that I don't care to witness. My advice is to
head up to the meadows alongside Highway 89 and fish for the brook-

ies and resident rainbows, or hike in to find the cutthroats. A stunning variety of wildflowers will be found here, too, particularly in a level meadow above the first falls, with deep-blue monkshood and orange lilies in abundance. As a bonus, the brook trout get larger than they do in many freestone creeks in the Sierra. This is a steeply falling, rocky little mountain stream, with brushy alders, willows, and logjams providing some cover. The few pools of any depth hold rainbows, plus cutthroats in the higher reaches, while the shallower runs hold the abundant brookies. There's no harm in taking a few of the latter for the frying pan back at camp. Mayflies, caddises, and Little Yellow Stoneflies are all present, but general fly patterns will work fine in the tumbling water.

To get to the Upper Truckee, take Highway 89 south from Meyers. Once past all the houses, you start to climb a grade, and in a mile, you'll see dirt roads on either side. Immediately after that, turn right onto the well-graded dirt road signposted to Upper Truckee Meadows. You'll wind downhill and cross the Upper Truckee. You can park before the bridge and fish up or downstream if you don't feel like hiking. If you do, turn left after the bridge, signposted to Hawley Grade Trail, and park before the end, being careful not to obstruct any driveways. Keep straight on to the trailhead, and just after another sign for the Hawley Grade Trail, an unmaintained trail heads to the left, alongside the stream. The Hawley Grade Trail leads uphill toward Echo Summit—it's not the one you want.

It's a steep hike for the first mile, then the trail goes to the right of a rocky outcrop and comes back to a thirty-foot falls. Above the falls, you'll come out onto a bench or shelf, and the going gets easier. In about half a mile, you'll see a grass lake, with some small ponds in it. The trail keeps right there, going up to Elbert Lake, which is a fine camping and fishing spot. There's only a faint trail beyond the lake, heading back downhill to the stream again. You might find it easier to follow the stream itself, though it's rough, marshy going for a while. If you keep going about a mile, to above Showers Creek, you'll be able to fish for the cutts exclusively. Now that the upper reaches are open, though, it's easier to get there on the Pacific Crest Trail from Highway 88 at Carson Pass, using the Caples Lake topo map to follow the trail.

In this area, **Meiss Lake** contains Lahontan cutthroats, but has been closed to all angling for several years. Check current regulations. **Showers Lake** has remained open. **Dardanelles, Elbert,** and **Round Lakes** contain plenty of brook trout.

TROUT CREEK
DeLorme: p. 90, B1–A1
USFS: Eldorado National Forest
USGS: South Lake Tahoe
Altitude: 8800–6200 feet
Water types: A little meadow stream with some undercuts and logs.
Trout: Rainbows, 6–9 inches; brook trout, 6–9 inches.
Special Regulations: Open for angling from July 1 to September 30.

The lower part of Trout Creek runs through narrow meadows edged with pine trees, right by a paved road through the suburbs of South Lake Tahoe. Despite the proximity of civilization, it's quite pretty in there. The stream has a sandy bed, with just a few deeper runs, fallen logs, and tree roots. Because of the comparative lack of cover, trout aren't abundant, but it's an interesting stalking challenge for the more experienced fly fisher, particularly one who's staying locally and can walk over after breakfast. Just don't expect any trophy fish. It can be reached farther up, where there are little rocky plunge pools, but alders cover it so densely that bait is the better fishing method up there—and it's not often that I'll say that.

From Highway 50 in Meyers, turn right at the stoplight onto Pioneer Trail. Past the housing tracts, you will see some gated four-wheel-drive tracks on the right. Park wherever you can and walk in to the creek, which runs parallel to the road.

SAXON CREEK
DeLorme: p. 90, B1–A1
USFS: Eldorado National Forest
USGS: South Lake Tahoe
Altitude: 8800–6400 feet
Water types: A tiny meadow stream with undercuts and logs.
Trout: Rainbows, 6–9 inches; brook trout, 6–9 inches.
Special Regulations: Open for angling from July 1 to September 30.

This tiny tributary of Trout Creek is similar to it, but with a little more cover for trout. From their junction up to a bridge, it is shaded by pine trees. Above the bridge, is a tough 200-yard slog through downed pines killed by bark beetles, but a trail on the right leads to a succession of meadows opening one after the other like a set of nesting boxes. Above the meadows is a boulder-filled canyon where the stream vanishes beneath the rocks, and above that, it's even tinier—and so are the brookies.

From Highway 50 in Meyers, turn right at the stop light onto Pioneer Trail. Take the fourth right onto Oneida Road, which becomes the paved Forest Road 1201. Park by the bridge where it crosses Saxon Creek.

GLEN ALPINE / TAYLOR CREEK
DeLorme: p. 89, A/B7
USFS: Eldorado National Forest
USGS: Emerald Bay
Altitude: 8800–6200 feet
Water types: Little pools with logs and tree roots for cover, pocket water.
Trout: Rainbows, 7–10 inches; browns, 8–11 inches; a few brook trout.
Special Regulations: Taylor Creek is open for angling from July 1 to September 30. There are no special regulations on Glen Alpine Creek.

This interesting stream is called Glen Alpine Creek above Fallen Leaf Lake, while below the lake, it's known as Taylor Creek. With its rocky bed and good cover, Taylor Creek is the principal spawning stream for Tahoe's kokanee salmon, and it also has runs of rainbows and browns. Victor Babbit, owner of Tahoe Fly Fishing Outfitters, is leading a campaign to get this stream declared a catch-and-release fishery. The Forest Service runs a nice visitor center on Taylor Creek, featuring a fascinating stream-observation chamber that was refurbished after the floods of 1997. Children will love the opportunity to observe a trout stream from below the waterline, and so should any fly fisher.

Above Fallen Leaf Lake, Glen Alpine Creek is formed from several steeply falling plunge-pool streams that drain lakes in the Desolation Wilderness. It flows across a fairly level bench, over a waterfall, across a second bench, and into weedy little Lily Lake. Then it flows over another waterfall and into Fallen Leaf Lake. The best fishing is on the benches or in the pocket water below the falls.

Heading north on Highway 89, turn left onto Fallen Leaf Road. Drive to the far end of the lake, to the trailhead parking lot, which can fill up early. The trail parallels the creek. You'll reach the second bench in a mile, before Glen Alpine Spring. The spring used to be the site of a resort, and its demise will be understood if you taste the sulfurous water. The trail reaches several lakes. (See the Desolation Wilderness listings.)

CASCADE CREEK
DeLorme: p. 89, A 6/7
USFS: Eldorado National Forest
USGS: Emerald Bay
Altitude: 7500–6200 feet
Water types: Little plunge pools and runs.
Trout: Brook trout, 5–8 inches; rainbows, 6–8 inches.
Special Regulations: Open below the lake for angling from July 1 to
September 30. There are no special regulations above the lake.

You may have read about the brook trout's propensity to overpopulate, and you could find no better place to see it in action. The larger pools (and I use "larger" as a relative term) will contain thirty tiny brookies, all ready to fight over your fly. That makes Cascade Creek an excellent place for the beginner to get his or her confidence boosted with a small dry fly—it probably won't matter which small dry fly. This tiny creek runs across a series of open granite benches, then over the falls that gives it its name, and then into Cascade Lake.

Head north on Highway 89, then turn left to the Bayview trailhead. Take the marked trail to Cascade Falls, and you'll find a faint trail going upstream, which can be tough to follow over bare granite and through some tangles of willow. It enters the Desolation Wilderness and will eventually lead to Azure Lake.

EAGLE CREEK
DeLorme: p. 89, A6/7
USFS: Eldorado National Forest
USGS: Emerald Bay
Altitude: 7000–6200 feet
Water types: Little pools, runs, and pocket water.
Trout: Rainbows, 7–9 inches; browns, 8–12 inches, plus a few brook trout.
Special Regulations: Open for angling from July 1 to September 30.

A short, but strenuous hike on the Eagle Falls Trail will bring you to Eagle Creek above the falls. When you first see the creek, it winds slowly over a sandy bed and holds a few spooky trout. Just upstream is an awful, impenetrable tangle of alders and huge logjams built by the spring runoff. If you can keep your temper, you might consider fighting your way into this jungle, because it hides some of the prettier brown trout you will ever see, with large spots of the deepest scarlet. Above the few pools behind the logjams, there's a brief stretch of pocket water before the lake, and some equally lovely rainbows and brookies with deep blood-red fins and a patch of scarlet on their bellies. I don't know what mineral causes this intense coloration, but it's worth fishing this stream once, just to see the fish.

Off Highway 89 heading north, turn left to the Eagle Falls trailhead. (There's a modest parking fee.) The trail enters the Desolation Wilderness, so you'll need a day permit.

MEEKS CREEK
DeLorme: p. 81, D6/7
USFS: Eldorado National Forest
USGS: Homewood
Altitude: 8100–6200 feet
Water types: Little pools and runs with log and tree-root cover.
Trout: Rainbows, 7–12 inches; brook trout, 6–10 inches;
browns, 7–12 inches.
Special Regulations: Open for angling from July 1 to September 30.

Where you cross Meeks Creek, it certainly doesn't look much of a fishery. Slow, silty meanders stretch back into the flat meadow. If you had a chainsaw, you could carve a way to the creek farther up the meadow, but all you would find is a sandy-bottomed spawning stream with tiny, spooky fish hiding wherever the tree roots provide some cover. But this is a stream of contrasts. At the end of the flat valley is a steeply falling section, below which is a short stretch of pocket water. And above the falls is a bench, where Meeks Creek winds through a fertile, marshy meadow with more cover than below. You'll have to do some serious brush busting to find a few places to make a cast, but the early-season hatches and the size of some of the trout might make it worthwhile. If you go in early July, be sure to take a Little Yellow Stone pattern, since there can be blizzards of the naturals then.

The trailhead is off Highway 89 at Meeks Bay, just north of the bridge over the creek. Get a day permit, since you'll probably enter the Desolation Wilderness. A mile hike will bring you to a logging spur on the left that leads to the falls. Stay right, and the trail climbs onto the bench, eventually leading to several lakes. (See the Desolation Wilderness listings.)

WARD CREEK
DeLorme: p. 81, C/D6
USFS: Tahoe National Forest
USGS: Tahoe City
Altitude: 7200–6200 feet
Water types: Little pools and rocky runs with tree-root cover.
Trout: Rainbows, 7–10 inches; brook trout, 6–9 inches.
Special Regulations: Open for angling from July 1 to September 30.

Most Tahoe shore streams fall steeply over granite benches, but Ward Creek runs through a shallow, forested canyon with a fairly even drop and provides some good trout habitat. An ongoing erosion control project should improve it further. However, since it has some of the only unimproved camping spots along the Tahoe shore, it sees a fair bit of fishing pressure. Groves of pines appear along the stream as it braids around small boulders, while small meadows slope down in places. Rainbow trout are fairly abundant, with brookies in the headwaters.

Turn off Highway 89 onto Pineland Road, which leads to Ward Creek Boulevard. This paved road parallels the creek for 2 miles, then a dirt road on the left leads farther upstream.

EAST PEAK LAKE
DeLorme: p. 90, A1
USFS: Toiyabe National Forest
USGS: South Lake Tahoe
Altitude: 8000 feet
Trout: Planted rainbows.

A private ten-acre fee fishery offering catch-and-release fly fishing, in the Heavenly Valley ski area. It offers fishing for large rainbow trout weighing as much as ten pounds. The lake is ideal for float tubing and limited to six anglers. Half-day and full-day tickets, guided only. Book through Tahoe Fly Fishing Outfitters at (530) 541-8208.

Blackwood Canyon and **Blackwood Creek** (see "Maybe Not . . ." immediately below) lead to **Barker Creek** and to **Bear** and **Miller Lakes**. (See the listings for the Middle Fork of the American River.)

MAYBE NOT . . .

On **Cold Creek** (DeLorme: p. 90, A1; USFS: Eldorado National Forest; USGS: South Lake Tahoe), between a housing tract and some aggressively posted private land, there's a mere half-mile of national forest land, heavily used by hikers and cyclists, the only part of this little Trout Creek tributary that you could fish. Worse yet, the stream is hidden in an impenetrable tangle of alder bushes, you'll get too hot in waders, and if you try to fish in shorts, you'll discover that it earns its name well. There are some small rainbows in Cold Creek, but I'd advise you not to bother. But the stream is open for angling from July 1 to September 30.

Tiny **Tallac Creek** (DeLorme: p. 89, A7; USFS: Eldorado National Forest; USGS: Emerald Bay) runs behind a housing tract. One branch drains Mount Tallac, while the other, Spring Creek, exits Floating Island Lake. If you can find nine inches of water, there'll be a nice brookie, but again, I'd advise you not to bother. Tallac Creek also is open for angling from July 1 to September 30.

Blackwood Canyon is the subject of a watershed improvement project, so Blackwood Creek may get better, but **General Creek, McKinney Creek,** and **Blackwood Creek,** all of which you may be tempted by when you pore over DeLorme: p. 81, D6; USFS: Tahoe; and USGS: Homewood, are so small, they all but dry up by fall. I'd abstain from trying to fish them, as well.

Lodging

It would be pointless to try to list all the many motels, cabins, bed and breakfasts, and luxury rentals available in South Lake Tahoe and along the Tahoe shore. Call the Visitors Authority or the Chamber of Commerce, and they'll send you a list.

Lake Tahoe Visitors Authority 1-800-822-5299

South Lake Tahoe Chamber of Commerce
(530) 541-5255

Tahoe City Chamber of Commerce (530) 583-2371

CAMPSITES

U.S. Forest Service campgrounds (USFS) have water and charge a fee, unless otherwise stated. Most cost a couple of dollars more per site than elsewhere in the Sierra. Private camps charge even more, but have showers. For USFS camps, marked with a telephone icon ☎, you can reserve a site by calling 1-800-280-CAMP. For state parks, marked with a telephone icon ☎, you can reserve a site by calling 1-800-444-7275.

Tahoe Pines
Highway 50
Private, showers
(530) 577-1653

KOA
Highway 50
Private, showers
(530) 577-3693

Campground by the Lake
South Lake Tahoe
City-run camp
Showers
(530) 542-6096

Tahoe Valley
South Lake Tahoe
Private, showers.
(530) 541-2222

Camp Richardson
Highway 89
Private, showers.
(530) 541-1801

Fallen Leaf ☎
Highway 89
USFS

Emerald Bay ☎
Highway 89
California State Park, showers.

Bayview
Highway 89
No fee, no water,
2-day limit, few sites

D. L. Bliss ☎
Highway 89
California State Park, showers.

Meeks Bay ☎
Highway 89
USFS

Meeks Bay Resort
Highway 89
Private, showers.
(530) 525-7242

Sugar Pine Point (R)
Highway 89
California State Park, showers.

Kaspian (r)
Highway 89
USFS

William Kent ☎
Highway 89
USFS.

Tahoe State Rec. Area
Tahoe City
California State Park, showers.

Lake Forest
Tahoe City
City-run camp
(530) 583-3796, x29

Undeveloped camping is a rarity along the Tahoe shore. You might find a site at the top of Trout Creek, behind South Lake Tahoe, or along Ward Creek, at the north end of the lake. With a backpack, though, the Desolation Wilderness is wide open.

FLY-FISHING SUPPLIES

Tahoe Fly Fishing Outfitters
3433 Lake Tahoe Boulevard
South Lake Tahoe CA, 96150
(530) 541-8208
Web site: www.tahoeflyfishing.com
A full-service fly shop.

OTHER SUPPLIES

Groceries and camping supplies are available in South Lake Tahoe, Homewood, Tahoma, Tahoe City, and at many of the resorts along the lakeshore. You can refill propane tanks at Bi-State Propane on James Avenue, east of the 50/89 intersection, or at the KOA campground on Highway 50.

Chapter 4: The Desolation Wilderness

Congress formally declared the Desolation Wilderness a wilderness area in 1969, though it was first protected from development way back in 1899, then designated as a roadless "primitive area" in 1931. Its sixty-three thousand acres provide one of the largest and most visited wildernesses in California. Its proximity to Lake Tahoe is one reason for its popularity, but the spectacular scenery and the stunning views it provides of the great lake are another, more powerful pull. Many people had their first backpacking experience here, so many that in 1978, it became necessary to limit visitors by a permit system to try to mitigate some of the worst effects of the crowds. That and the more recent campfire ban have started to return this wilderness to something a little closer to its natural state.

Upper Velma Lake, Desolation Wilderness. Early evening is the prime time to fish this stillwater.

The Desolation Wilderness contains over a hundred small to medium-sized lakes in granitic basins scoured out by glacial activity. The only native trout are rainbows, found in the Rubicon River and a few lakes in the center of the wilderness, and Lahontan cutthroats that had spread from Lake Tahoe into Fallen Leaf and a few nearby lakes. Long before the area was declared a wilderness, many lakes were raised by low dams to improve their fish-holding capacity and maintain some year-round stream flow to help trout spawn. Haphazard trout planting started in the late 1800s, spreading them to formerly barren lakes, and the Department of Fish and Game began aerial planting in the 1950s. Today, brookies are the most abundant trout, aided by their ability to spawn successfully in lakes that lack an inflow stream. Rainbows are planted in many lakes and are the second most numerous trout species, while the state fish, the beautiful golden trout, exists in some of the higher, more remote waters. Wild brown trout are found wherever conditions are right for spawning in the fall, and a few cutthroats have been planted in the past.

Getting there shortly after the ice melts can provide some of the best fishing of the season. Victor Babbit, of Tahoe Fly Fishing Outfitters, says that ice-out starts between mid-May and mid-July, depending on the weather and the elevation. As a general rule, in a year with a reasonably warm spring, lakes at 6500 feet, about the lowest elevation in the Desolation Wilderness, will be clear by mid-May. Those at 8000 feet will take until mid-June. A cold, late spring can delay ice-out by up to a month. You should also bear in mind that lakes that are open to the south will thaw faster than those that have high mountains to shade them. Small lakes that nestle under north-facing slopes may scarcely thaw at all in a cold year.

Ten major trailheads provide access to the Desolation Wilderness, and they're listed below. If you don't want to camp overnight, quite a few lakes are within a strenuous day's hike, though they do see the most fishing pressure. For day use, you fill out a free permit at the trailhead. If you're staying overnight between June 15 and Labor Day, you have to obtain a permit from one of the National Forest Service offices. Half the permits can be booked up to ninety days in advance from the Eldorado National Forest Information Center, while the other half are available only on the day they're used (see below). The center also sells the map that you'll need, the U.S. Forest Service *Guide to the Desolation Wilderness*, with 2-inches-to-the-mile detail and forty-foot contour intervals, which covers the

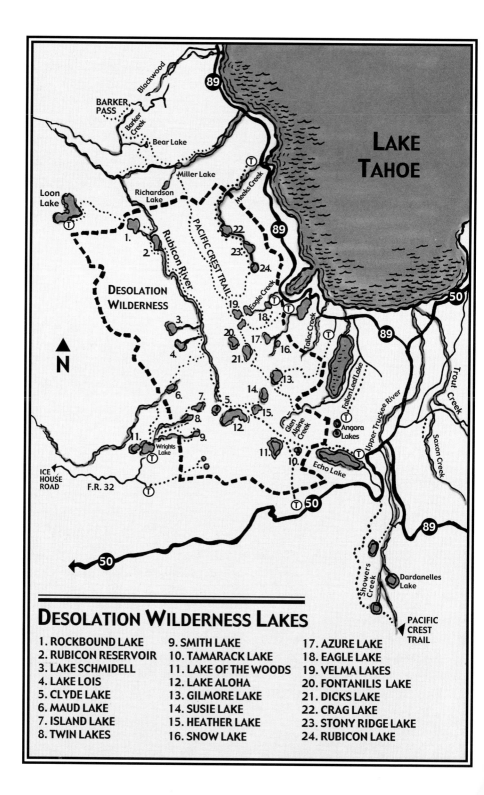

Desolation Wilderness Lakes

1. ROCKBOUND LAKE	9. SMITH LAKE	17. AZURE LAKE
2. RUBICON RESERVOIR	10. TAMARACK LAKE	18. EAGLE LAKE
3. LAKE SCHMIDELL	11. LAKE OF THE WOODS	19. VELMA LAKES
4. LAKE LOIS	12. LAKE ALOHA	20. FONTANILIS LAKE
5. CLYDE LAKE	13. GILMORE LAKE	21. DICKS LAKE
6. MAUD LAKE	14. SUSIE LAKE	22. CRAG LAKE
7. ISLAND LAKE	15. HEATHER LAKE	23. STONY RIDGE LAKE
8. TWIN LAKES	16. SNOW LAKE	24. RUBICON LAKE

Desolation Wilderness very well. If you decide to use topo maps, you'll need Homewood, Rockbound Valley, Emerald Bay, Pyramid Peak, and Echo Lake to cover the whole area. Note: No campfires are allowed, and you must get a fire permit for your gas stove.

To Make Advance Reservations and Pick Up Permits
Eldorado National Forest Information Center
3070 Camino Heights Drive
Camino, CA 95709
(530) 644-6048
Off Highway 50, east of Placerville.

To Pick Up Permits Only
Lake Tahoe Basin Management Unit Office
870 Emerald Bay Road
South Lake Tahoe, CA 96150
(530) 573-2600
On Highway 89, just north of junction with Highway 50.

Lake Tahoe Visitor Center
Highway 89
South Lake Tahoe, CA 96150
(530) 573-2674
Off Highway 89 on right, 3 miles north of South Lake Tahoe.

Desolation Wilderness Lakes

The lakes marked with a star symbol (★) could all be considered within a day hike, allowing time to fish, but only if you're fit. Many will take an energetic hiker as much as three hours to reach. The rest are certainly overnight venues, few of which I have fished.

Fallen Leaf Lake · Glen Alpine Trailhead
Off Highway 89 · 6600 feet elevation

Grass Lake ★ · 2-mile hike · 7200 feet elevation
Brown, brook, and rainbow trout. Heavily fished, and the weedy margins make it tough to cast.

Gilmore Lake ★ · 4-mile hike · 8300 feet elevation
A large lake with mostly lake trout, but some brookies, browns, and rainbows, too. A float tube is an advantage.

Susie Lake ★ · 4-mile hike · 7800 feet elevation
Brook trout and rainbows, possibly browns. Rocky points provide casting room.

Heather Lake ★ · 5-mile hike · 7900 feet elevation
Brook and brown trout, and both can get large, probably because of the minnows found here. A few rainbows, as well.

Half Moon Lake ★ · 5-mile hike · 8200 feet elevation
Brook trout and rainbows. Shallow shorelines make waders or a float tube useful.

Tallac Trailhead
Off Highway 8 · 6400 feet elevation

Floating Island Lake ★ · 1-mile hike · 7200 feet elevation
Brookies, some quite large, inhabit this fertile little lake and spawn in the outflow stream. It's surrounded by trees, so there's more casting room if you have waders.

Cathedral Lake ★ · 2-mile hike · 7600 feet elevation
Golden trout are planted in this tiny lake, but can be tough to catch. There is casting room on the steep bank on the far side. This is a sort of highway rest stop for the many hikers who climb Mount Tallac for the view, so expect swimmers, dogs retrieving sticks, and other spectacles. Of course this spooks the fish, so it's best to be there very early.

BAYVIEW TRAILHEAD
JUST OFF HIGHWAY 89 · 6900 FEET ELEVATION

GRANITE LAKE ★ · 1-MILE (STEEP) HIKE · 7700 FEET ELEVATION
A small, heavily wooded lake with brookies. A float tube
helps a lot.

AZURE LAKE ★ · 2-MILE (STEEP) HIKE · 7700 FEET ELEVATION
Better reached from the Eagle Falls Trail (see the listing for
the next trailhead), since the Bayview Trail climbs very steeply to
8400 feet before descending again.

SNOW LAKE ★ · 2-MILE OFF-TRAIL HIKE · 7400 FEET ELEVATION
A medium-sized lake with lots of small brook trout. There is no
formal trail, so you have to follow the faint track from Cascade
Falls (signposted at the trailhead) up Cascade Creek.

EAGLE FALLS TRAILHEAD
ALONGSIDE HIGHWAY 89 · 6600 FEET ELEVATION

EAGLE LAKE ★ · 1-MILE (STEEP) HIKE · 7000 FEET ELEVATION
Browns, rainbows, and brookies, some fairly large. A fairly
heavily fished small lake. A float tube would be a distinct
advantage, since there's little casting room.

AZURE LAKE ★ · 2-MILE (STEEP) HIKE · 7700 FEET ELEVATION
This spectacular, medium-sized lake in a steep-sided granite bowl
holds brook trout, which can get quite large. I've caught a lovely
11-inch golden here, too, but that's a real rarity. It probably came
down from Kalmia Lake, where they are planted. Contains
Callibaetis mayflies and damsels. The trail climbs fairly steeply to
8200 feet before descending again. Take the Bayview Trail to the
left. In 500 yards, an unmarked trail descends a rocky gully on the
right, just after you round a shoulder. Don't head downhill when you
first see the lake, because you will run into impassable cliffs and an
impenetrable jungle.

UPPER VELMA LAKE ★ · 3-MILE (STEEP) HIKE · 7900 FEET ELEVATION
Both it and a narrow little lakelet below contain plenty of brookies and
rainbows and have good casting spots. The connecting stream is good early
in the season.

LOWER VELMA LAKE ★ · 4-MILE (STEEP) HIKE · 7700 FEET ELEVATION
There are brookies, rainbows, and browns in this lake, some quite large,
and reasonable spots to cast from, but many steep cliffs, too. It has an inflow
stream for spawning.

MIDDLE VELMA LAKE ★ · 4-MILE (STEEP) HIKE · 7900 FEET ELEVATION
Illogically, this medium-sized lake isn't connected to either Upper or Lower
Velma. It has no spawning stream, so the rainbows are grown from fingerlings planted by air, and some get quite large. The lake has plenty of
rocky promontories to cast from, and is quite fertile.

FONTANILIS LAKE ★ · 4 1/2-MILE (STEEP) HIKE · 8300 FEET ELEVA-
TION
There are mostly brook trout, with some rainbows, in this medium-
sized lake. Fair casting spots are available.

DICKS LAKE ★ · 4-MILE (STEEP) HIKE · 8400 FEET ELEVATION
It's mostly brookies, with some rainbows, in this largish lake in a steep
granite bowl.

MEEKS CREEK TRAILHEAD
ALONGSIDE HIGHWAY 89 · 6200 FEET ELEVATION

GENEVIEVE LAKE ★ · 4 1/2-MILE HIKE · 7400 FEET ELEVATION
A small, heavily wooded lake with brookies and some browns. A float tube
would help a lot, since the shorelines are shallow.

CRAG LAKE ★ · 5-MILE HIKE · 7500 FEET ELEVATION
Brown trout are the main species here and get quite large dining on minnows. They're often tough to catch. Some casting room.

HIDDEN LAKE ★ · 5 1/2-MILE HIKE · 7500 FEET ELEVATION
A little lake just off the main trail. Contains brookies and has rocky points
for casting room.

SHADOW LAKE ★ · 5 1/2-MILE HIKE · 7600 FEET ELEVATION
A small, shallow lake with some sizable brook trout, plus a few rainbows and browns.

STONY RIDGE LAKE · 6 1/2-MILE HIKE · 7800 FEET ELEVATION
A large, very deep lake with brook, brown, and rainbow trout. Lake trout were once planted here, too. Casting is possible from the shore, but a float tube would be better.

RUBICON LAKE · 7 1/2-MILE HIKE · 8300 FEET ELEVATION
A small lake with brook trout.

GROUSE LAKES · 8-MILE HIKE · 8200 FEET ELEVATION
These are tiny lakes, particularly the lower one. A spur trail goes to the upper lake first. Both have casting room and contain brookies.

PHIPPS LAKE · 9-MILE HIKE · 8600 FEET ELEVATION
Just off the main trail. Good fishing for brookies, and some goldens have been planted. Some casting room is available.

LOON LAKE TRAILHEAD
FROM HIGHWAY 50 · VIA ICE HOUSE ROAD, FOREST ROAD 3 · 6600 FEET ELEVATION

Note that the last six of these lakes and the upper Rubicon River are closer to other trailheads, particularly to the Wrights Lake / Twin Lakes Trailhead, but a lot less climbing is involved from Loon Lake. It's also possible to reach Buck Island Lake by jeep from Wentworth Springs, which would shorten these hikes by 6 miles.

ROCKBOUND LAKE · 6 1/2-MILE HIKE · 6400 FEET ELEVATION
A large lake with brookies, rainbows, and browns.

RUBICON RESERVOIR · 8-MILE HIKE · 6500 FEET ELEVATION
A large, man-made lake that dammed the Rubicon River and reduced the free-flowing section of the river to 10 miles. Contains rainbows, brookies, and browns.

Rubicon River • 9 1/2-mile hike• 6600 feet elevation
Above the reservoir is the last truly wild section of this river. It contains mostly rainbows in the lower part of this section, while the headwaters contain golden trout that moved down from Clyde Lake. Hybrids between the two will be found, as well.

4-Q's Lakes • 14 1/2-mile hike • 7500 feet elevation
Horseshoe Lake • 16 1/2-mile hike• 7600 feet elevation
Zitella Lake • 17-mile hike • 7700 feet elevation
Brookies inhabit all three of these small, shallow lakes. Rainbows have been caught in Horseshoe.

Highland Lake • 18-mile hike • 7800 feet elevation
There are rainbow trout in this medium-sized lake, some fairly large, some wild.

McConnell Lake • 18-mile hike • 7800 feet elevation
Leland Lakes • 19-mile hike • 8200 feet elevation
These small lakes receive plantings of goldens.

Dark Lake • (Rockbound Trailhead)
From Highway 50, via Ice House Road, Forest Road 3 • 7000 feet elevation

These lakes are reached via the Barrett Lake Jeep Trail, which can of course be driven by jeep. All the lakes listed under the Wrights Lake / Twin Lakes Trailhead can also be reached from here.

Barrett Lake ★ • 5-mile hike • 7600 feet elevation
This small lake is just outside the Desolation Wilderness, but is not fished too much. It does provide good numbers of brook trout and some rainbows.

Lawrence Lake ★ • 5 1/2-mile hike • 7800 feet elevation
Brookies here, some fairly large. The stream from Top Lake is the most significant inflow.

Top Lake ★ · 6-mile hike · 8100 feet elevation
There are some sizable brookies in this lake, and some goldens. There is a trail to Top Lake from Lawrence Lake, although it isn't formally maintained, so it's not on the map.

Wrights Lake · (Twin Lakes Trailhead)
From Highway 50, via Ice House Road,
Forest Road 3 · 7000 feet elevation

Maud Lake ★ · 4-mile hike · 7700 feet elevation
Wild brown trout, with some rainbows and brookies. Much of the lake is shallow, but the far end provides deep water, while the shallows provide food. The inlet stream has undercut banks, which can offer good fishing when the stream flows strongly.

Lake Lois · 6 1/2-mile hike · 8300 elevation
The first worthwhile lake you reach after going through Rockbound Pass at 8550 feet. You'll find brookies in this open lake and rocky points for casting.

Lake Schmidell · 7 1/2-mile hike · 7900 feet elevation
There are plenty of brookies in this large, deep lake, and good casting spots.

Gertrude Lake ★ · 4-mile hike · 8000 feet elevation
This small lake is stocked with golden trout, but also contains brookies.

Tyler Lake ★ · 4-mile hike · 8200 feet elevation
A little lake with brookies.

Twin Lakes ★ · 2 1/2-mile hike · 8000 feet elevation
Brookies and some rainbows here, some fairly large. Plenty of casting room.

Island Lake ★ · 3-mile hike · 8200 feet elevation
Brookies and goldens. A medium-sized lake in a rocky basin. Good casting room.

Maud Lake, Twin Lakes Trailhead.

GROUSE LAKE ★ · 2-MILE HIKE · 8200 FEET ELEVATION
A little lake with brookies and some rainbows. Not much casting room.

HEMLOCK LAKE ★ · 2-MILE HIKE · 8400 FEET ELEVATION
A brushy, tiny lake with small brookies.

SMITH LAKE ★ · 2 1/2-MILE HIKE · 8700 FEET ELEVATION
A pretty, high alpine lake with lots of brookies.

LYONS CREEK TRAILHEAD
FROM HIGHWAY 50, VIA ICE HOUSE ROAD,
FOREST ROAD 3 · 6700 FEET ELEVATION

LYONS LAKE ★ · 5-MILE HIKE · 8400 FEET ELEVATION
There are brookies, including some fairly large ones, in this small-to-medium-sized lake.

SYLVIA LAKE ★ · 5-MILE HIKE · 8100 FEET ELEVATION
This is smaller than Lyons Lake, and so are the abundant brookies. It has adequate casting room.

Azure Lake, Eagle Falls Trailhead.

Echo Lake Trailhead
Just off Highway 50 · 7400 feet elevation

Note that all of these lakes can be reached just as easily from Ralston Trailhead, but it's about the same distance and adds a rather unnecessary 900 feet to the climb.

There is also a water taxi available at Echo Lake, which could cut 2 1/2 miles off these hiking distances.

Tamarack Lake ★ · 3 1/2-mile hike · 7800 feet elevation
There are brookies, including some fairly large ones, in this medium-sized lake.

Ralston Lake ★ · 4-mile hike · 7800 feet elevation
Small, abundant brookies. Adequate casting room, but steep cliffs.

Lake of the Woods ★ · 5-mile hike · 8100 feet elevation
Three are brookies and rainbows in this medium-sized lake, and both get fairly large.

Ropi Lake • 7-mile hike • 7600 feet elevation
Toem Lake • 7 1/2-mile hike • 7600 feet elevation
Two small lakes with good brook trout fishing and good casting room.

Desolation Lake • 6-mile hike • 8000 feet elevation
Channel Lake • 6 1/2-mile hike • 8100 feet elevation
American Lake • 7-mile hike • 8100 feet elevation
Another chain of good brookie lakes, connected to Ropi Lake by a stream that also offers good fishing. Some rainbows may be found in all these lakes. This is a particularly attractive area.

Waca Lake• 7 1/2-mile hike• 8200 feet elevation
Pyramid Lake • 8-mile hike• 8100 feet elevation
More small lakes with brookies, best reached via American Lake.

Lake Lucille ★ • 5-mile hike • 8200 feet elevation
Lake Margery ★ • 5-mile hike • 8200 feet elevation
Two small, shallow lakes with some small brook trout.

Lake Aloha • 6-mile hike • 8100 feet elevation
Aloha appears to be huge on the map, but it was created by a PG&E dam, so it shrinks as the summer passes and they use the water. It contains brookies and rainbows, though.

Lake Le Conte • 6 1/2-mile hike • 8200 feet elevation
A small lake in a granite bowl, and not very fertile. It has brookies and rainbows.

Clyde Lake • 9-mile hike 8100 • feet elevation
This lake is the source of the Rubicon River. Golden trout inhabit it and have spread downriver. Reached through Mosquito Pass at 8400 feet, it also can be reached from the Twin Lakes Trailhead at Wrights lake, a 9 1/2-mile hike, or from the Glen Alpine Trailhead at Fallen Leaf Lake, an 8-mile hike.

TRIANGLE LAKE ★ • 4-MILE HIKE • 8400 FEET ELEVATION
There are rainbows and brookies in this small, weedy, and fertile lake. A float tube helps.

LAKES JUST OUTSIDE THE DESOLATION WILDERNESS

ANGORA LAKES • 1/2-MILE HIKE • 7400 FEET ELEVATION
Reached from Fallen Leaf Lake by turning left to Tahoe Mountain, then right to Angora Lookout, Angora Lake is planted with Lahontan cutthroats.

QUAIL LAKE • DRIVE-TO • 7100 FEET ELEVATION
A private, sixteen-acre fee fishery offering catch-and-release fly fishing only. Quail Lake has large planted rainbows weighing as much as eight pounds. The lake is ideal for float tubing and limited to four anglers. It's in the Homewood ski area and operated by Mountaintop Management. Call (530) 525-5676 for details and reservations.

CHAPTER 5: THE TRUCKEE RIVER AREA

Situated just to the north of the Lake Tahoe basin, the town of Truckee is a popular tourist destination in its own right. The population is growing rapidly, and to nobody's surprise, the number of anglers fishing local waters is also on the increase. People throng Truckee-area waters in the late spring and throughout most of the summer. So if there is a place in the Sierra where the rules of angling etiquette need to be strictly observed, the Truckee River is it. And we could probably add Martis Creek Reservoir, the Little Truckee River, and several other local streams to the list.

This doesn't mean you can't find good fishing near or even in the town of Truckee. The hatches on these east-slope waters can have an intensity that would surprise anyone who fishes the west slope of the Sierra, and although the average size of the trout might not be all that impressive, some truly big 'uns are waiting to engulf a well-placed dry fly or a deeply dredged nymph or streamer. Expect company, though, and be generous of your time and space while fishing the Truckee area.

Truckee River, Glenshire Drive. This well-known river flows east into Nevada, and offers challenging angling and lots of competition.

THE TRUCKEE RIVER

DeLorme: p. 81, C6–A7
USFS: Tahoe National Forest
USGS: Tahoe City, Truckee, Martis Peak, Boca
Altitude: 6200–5200 feet
Water types: Pools, riffles, and some pocket water.
Trout: Rainbows, 9–20 inches; browns, 9–22 inches, some
bigger; a few whitefish.
Special Regulations: Trout Creek to Glenshire Bridge and
Prosser Creek to Boca Bridge: two trout, minimum size 15 inches,
only artificial lures with barbless hooks. Glenshire Bridge to
Prosser Creek (mostly private water): as above, but fly fishing only.
Boca Bridge to Gray Creek: two trout, minimum size 15 inches.

If the Truckee River could be magically lifted from its valley and transported to Montana, it surely would be added to the pantheon of nationally recognized trout streams. The truth, though, is that it's hardly known outside California or Nevada. There could be many reasons for this, but the main one could be the very nature of the valley in which it sits—the most heavily used route through the Sierra Nevada, traversed by both Interstate 80 and the railway line to Reno. To describe the river as overly scenic requires a selective focus that blocks out some of the surroundings and dims the roar of the freeway. The Truckee sees quite a bit of fishing pressure, too, but the size of the wild trout that are caught can make it all worthwhile.

The river flows out of Lake Tahoe through a Bureau of Reclamation dam that controls the flow—originally for ranchers in Nevada, not trout, though that is changing. The recent Truckee River Operating Agreement enabled federal and state agencies to buy back water rights for many uses, including restoration of the Lahontan cutthroat trout in Pyramid Lake. Ralph Cutter, author of the Sierra Trout Guide, tells me that the diversion dam at Floriston washed out in 1997 and won't be rebuilt without a fish ladder. If fish ladders can be added to three other dams, then wild Lahontan cutthroats might spawn in the river once again.

For the first 3.5 miles, the Truckee meanders through shallow riffles and runs, then slowly over a silt bed with little weed growth. There's not much cover for trout there, so most of the fish are juveniles, the progeny of spawning runs from downstream. Another good reason for avoiding this section is the heavy raft traffic. On a hot summer day, you can

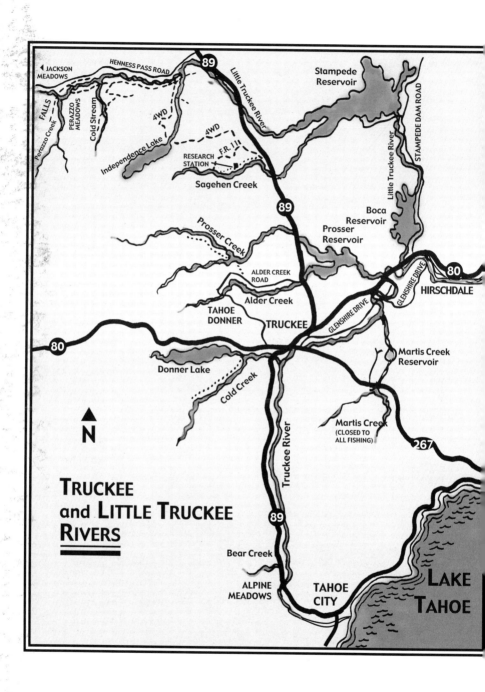

TRUCKEE
and LITTLE TRUCKEE
RIVERS

hardly find space to make a cast, so it's no surprise that the larger fish will be in hiding. The rafts take out at River Ranch Lodge, though, by the confluence with Bear Creek. A mile of pocket water begins there, continuing to the turnoff to Squaw Valley. From there downstream to Donner Creek, the river is mostly riffles and shallow runs, with an occasional pool. Throughout this upper 12 miles, the river is paralleled by Highway 89, and it's never more than a short stroll from pullout to riverbank. The fishing pressure is considerable, as a result, and many of the trout will be planted rainbows, but don't think that's all that lives there. Wild browns and rainbows can be caught without the fishing being quite as picky as it is downstream, in the designated Wild Trout section of the river.

The river swings eastward just before its confluence with Donner Creek. Through the city of Truckee, there's some interesting pocket water along South River Street, though the surroundings are hardly scenic. The Wild Trout section starts at the junction with Trout Creek, just east of town. Along Glenshire Drive, the river flows quickly in riffles and runs between sagebrush hills, with a narrow riparian zone of willows and cottonwoods. Then, at Glenshire Bridge, it begins to enter a broad canyon and meanders once again. The fishing is private for a short section downstream of the bridge, the property belonging to the San Francisco Flycasters as far as the first I-80 bridge, just before Prosser Creek. At the next "S" bend, after the second I-80 bridge, are two pools, the deep one under the dirt cliff being known as Horner's Corner, after Jack Horner, the inventor of the Horner Deer Hair Fly—perhaps better known today as the Humpy. The river passes under Interstate 80 for the third time, then runs quite straight through a half-mile or so of continuous pocket water to its confluence with the Little Truckee at Boca. The flow is increased substantially here, particularly in midsummer, when water is being released from Stampede and Boca Reservoirs to satisfy irrigation demands in Nevada.

At Hirschdale, the Truckee enters a deeper canyon, and it's here that the river starts to become a little wilder in character. The only access downstream is by foot, along the railroad line, until the small town of Floriston, 7 miles down I-80. There are large pools both above and below Hirschdale Bridge, and some of the largest brown trout live in this canyon, below hills clad in pine and juniper, hiding in dark, swirling water or in steady, deep glides that sweep against the riprap of the railroad line. This part of the river can be tough to fish in the summer because of the heavy flows, but in the fall, it's entirely different. It's scenic then, too, as cottonwoods and aspens turn to golden shades along the grassy banks while the blood-red leaves of wild roses clothe the steeper slopes.

Department of Fish and Game surveys in 1993 found an average of more than eighteen hundred trout per mile in the Wild Trout section, a figure that's still steadily increasing from the drought of the early 1990s. Browns are slightly more numerous than wild rainbows, and browns over 15 inches, which are found throughout the river, are more common than rainbows of that size. Though both species grow to over 20 inches, the average trout you're likely to catch is between 10 and 12. In 2002, the U.S. Fish and Wildlife Service began an ambitious project to restore Lahontan cutthroat to the drainage. These fish had been extinct in the river since the 1930s.

Fishing methods on the Truckee run the gamut from the use of tiny dries, matching the Blue-Winged Olives, to outsized streamers that imitate the crayfish and minnows of the lower river. As Frank Pisciotta, a local guide, tells all his customers, if there's one consistently successful method, it's swinging soft-hackle wet flies, probably because emerging caddisflies are the most common item in the trouts' diet. Many fly fishers on the Truckee stick entirely to indicator nymph fishing, though, which can be highly successful. If that's your choice, the Bird's Nest is a favorite pattern, with a Prince or similar peacock-bodied nymph a close second. Large fish can be caught on the surface, though, as long as the angler is prepared to switch between emerger, soft-hackle, and cripple patterns. This is not to say that a high-floating dry doesn't work, but the fish see plenty of feathered frauds to compare and contrast with natural insects, so they're not easily fooled by attractors like the Royal Wulff.

The best dry-fly action comes when the hatching caddises are on the water with egg-laying Little Yellow Stoneflies. These stoneflies can be surprisingly prolific on a summer evening, and one of the several different species involved is a chunky size 12 insect that causes explosive rises by fluttering on the surface. Twitch or skate your imitation to bring the same result, using a small Yellow Stimulator or an Elk Hair Caddis. During caddis time, you should always get ready to tie on a soft hackle or a LaFontaine Emergent Sparkle Pupa at the end of the evening. Mayfly hatches are less significant on the Truckee, though sparse Green Drakes in the early season can bring up big trout like nothing else. They share

TRUCKEE RIVER HATCH TABLE

Insect	Dates	Size
March Brown (Rithrogena)	May–June	12–14
Blue Winged Olive (Baetis)	May–June mid-September–mid-November	16–20 18–22
Pale Morning Dun	June–mid-July	16–18
Creamy-Orange Dun (Serratella aka Ephemerella tibialis)	mid-June–mid-August	6
Green Drake (Drunella aka Ephemerella doddsi, grandis ingens, grandis grandis)	mid-June	10–12
Tricos (Tricorythodes)	mid-September–October	20–22
Spotted Sedge (Hydropsyche)	mid-May–mid-August	12–16
Green Sedge (Rhyacophila)	mid-May–July	10–14
Saddle-Case Caddis (Glossosoma)	July–August	16–18
October Caddis (Dicosmoecus)	October–November	6–8
Little Yellow Stonefly (Isoperla)	mid-May–mid-July	12–16
Golden Stonefly	mid-May–mid-June	6–8
Midges	All season	20–24

the water with some big Golden Stones, which are not particularly prolific here, either, though their size makes a large Orange Stimulator worth a try. In midsummer, it's not out of the question to raise trout with a grasshopper pattern, particularly anywhere near a grassy bank, since the naturals will be hopping around in numbers by then.

The best of the summer mayfly hatches seems to be a creamy-orange-colored dun also found on the Yuba system. Ralph Cutter, who knows this river so much better than I do, has identified it as *Ephemerella tibialis*—also known nowadays as *Serratella tibialis,* since a lot of mayflies have been reclassified and given different names by entomologists using DNA, not the old-fashioned eyeball-and-microscope method, to the further confusion of Latin-weary anglers. Being of the Ephemerellidae family of crawler nymphs, it's a chunky-bodied insect that takes quite a while to hatch, since none of the family swims well, making the emergers important both to the trout and to the angler. The fall probably provides the most consistent dry-fly action with mayfly patterns, though. The *Baetis* or Blue-Winged Olive hatch starts around noon and provides good fishing for two hours. This can easily be extended to a whole day by fishing Pheasant Tail Soft Hackles and Pheasant Tail Nymphs before and after the hatch.

Finally, there is no question that the best chance of a really large fish from the Truckee comes with the use of streamer patterns. The browns in this river don't get as big as they do by nibbling on midges. In case you're wondering just how big they get, Ralph Cutter videotaped a 31-inch brown while diving in the Truckee in 1997. The river contains plenty of sculpins, a mess of dace and suckers, and lots of crayfish to feed those hearty appetites. Ralph recommends Woolly Buggers, Clouser Minnows in a green-and-orange color scheme, and his own pattern, the Goblin, as streamers, all of which imitate crayfish quite well.

For access, Highway 89 runs along the upper 12 miles of the Truckee, from Lake Tahoe to Donner Creek. There are pullouts throughout this stretch, and a paved bicycle path runs along the river from Tahoe City to River Ranch. If you want to fish the stretch west of the town of Truckee, turn south on Highway 267, cross the railroad line, and take the first right onto South River Street, which immediately turns to dirt and heads upstream for 2 miles, though it's not suitable for passenger cars after the first half-mile.

The Wild Trout section, which tends to be very heavily fished, starts at Trout Creek. Drive through Truckee and turn right onto Glenshire Drive after you leave town. There are three pullouts on your right at 1.3 miles, 1.9 miles and 2.3 miles. From all of these pullouts, you cross the railroad line and hike across level sagebrush flats for a couple of hundred yards to the river. The road crosses the river at Glenshire Bridge, where there is a large parking area on your right on the far side of the bridge. You can also take the last Truckee exit off Interstate 80, signposted to 89 North, head toward Truckee, and you'll see Glenshire Drive on your left. Glenshire Drive heads uphill after the bridge, away from the river for a while.

The next downstream access is directly off I-80. As you head downhill, 4.9 miles after the Highway 89 North exit, turn right onto a dirt road just after you cross the river for the second time. There are several parking spots there, and the water at this "S" bend includes the pool called Horner's Corner. If you head upstream, under the freeway bridge, you can walk the railroad line for a mile or so to the previous freeway bridge, known as Union Mills Bridge, which is the downstream boundary of the private water. You'll cross Prosser Creek and see plenty of deep runs to fish on the way back.

The next access is at Boca Bridge. Exit the freeway for Hirschdale and Boca, then turn left to Boca. You'll cross the river and see an open parking area on the right. Cross the road and walk up the railroad line, past the outflow of the Little Truckee River. This is the lower end of a mile of good pocket water. If you turn right to Hirschdale, you'll be on Glenshire Drive again, heading back toward Truckee. In less than half a mile, you'll come to a fork where Hirschdale Road goes left to the small hamlet of Hirschdale. Cross the bridge, park on the left, and you can walk the railroad line either upstream or downstream. It's 4 miles to Gray Creek. This stretch was severely burned by a forest fire during the summer of 2001. Be careful when choosing your route down, since the railroad embankment is frequently steep and composed of loose clinker. Note that the road continues beyond the bridge, but dead-ends in private property, which you should not attempt to enter.

BEAR CREEK
DeLorme: p. 81, C6.
USFS: Tahoe National Forest
USGS: Tahoe City
Altitude: 7200–6000 feet
Water types: Little pools and runs.
Trout: Rainbows, 7–10 inches; brook trout, 8–10 inches.

A few rainbows hide wherever there is any cover in the lower reaches of Bear Creek, but the flow drops to a trickle by midsummer. It's not a bad place for the beginner in early season, though, with the stream meandering through an open flood plain. Upstream, through the Alpine Meadows ski resort, the stream is hemmed in by brush, and this makes it difficult to fish with a fly.

Deer Creek and Deep Creek also produce some small rainbow trout. All three of these streams are easily accessed off Highway 89. **Pole Creek** is closed to all angling to protect a breeding population of Lahontan cutthroats that the Department of Fish and Game has established there. As for **Squaw Creek,** there was a recent radio ad that went something like "Ski Squaw Valley and prepare to be impressed." Well, the slogan for the stream should be "Fish Squaw Valley and prepare to be appalled." When I fished it, the water appeared to be used up by the golf course and resort, leaving a trickle for the very few little trout that clung on somehow. The stream was full of crushed soda cans, so I carried out all I could find, marveling at the mentality of a litterbug who apparently could go to the trouble of meticulously flattening them with his boot heel, but not the lesser trouble of carrying them out in his pocket. And this meadow stream was once the home of some really big brown trout, too. Now it's a tragedy and a disgrace.

COLD CREEK
DeLorme: p. 81, B5–B6
USFS: Tahoe National Forest
USGS: Norden, Truckee
Altitude: 7500–5700 feet
Water types: A little meadow stream with pools and runs, some pocket water.
Trout: Rainbows, 7–11 inches; browns, 9–11 inches; brook trout, 7–9 inches.

Cold Creek, also known as Cold Stream Creek, runs through a broad, 3-mile-long valley just behind Shallenberger Ridge, which you see towering above Donner Lake from Highway 80. This pretty valley used to be in private hands, but it was bought by the state, and now it's part of Donner Memorial State Park. A lot of gravel extraction went on here, but the damage to the watershed is gradually being restored. First you'll come to a stretch of pocket water, not a bad place for the beginner to fish. Upstream, you'll find a rather degraded meadow stream with too wide a channel, best fished early in the season because of the lack of cover and sometimes because of lack of water. Wherever there are tree roots or logs, though, there are sizable trout, mainly rainbows. Of course, they're spooky, which means casting over the gravel bars with long, fine leaders, but the farther you go, the better the fishing gets. This stream would be a pleasant challenge for the older angler, since it's a fairly level hike.

To get there, turn off Interstate 80 at the Donner Park exit, then stay straight across toward the Chevron station. Bear right and park by the locked barrier, then hike the old road as far as you want to go. Eventually, you'll reach a posted private inholding, where you'll have to continue in the streambed.

MARTIS CREEK RESERVOIR
DeLorme: p. 81, B6/7
USFS: Tahoe National Forest
USGS: Truckee
Altitude: 5800 feet
Trout: Planted and wild rainbows, wild browns, and Lahontan cutthroats.
Special Regulations: Catch-and-release, artificial lures with barbless hooks only.

Martis Creek Reservoir is a very fertile, seventy-acre water-supply reservoir surrounded by sagebrush flats in an open valley south of Truckee. It was California's very first lake to become part of the Wild Trout Program and was once reserved for Lahontan cutthroat trout. The trouble with that plan, though, was that the wild brown trout from Martis Creek kept repopulating the lake, so it became one of the best brown trout fisheries in California. Then the Department of Fish and Game began to stock it with rainbows, instead, and this coincided with a decline in the browns, probably caused by the drought of the early 1990s. Now Lahontan cutthroats are being planted again, so there should soon be some large ones among the rainbows, which often are as big as 18 inches. There are even larger trout than that though, including some seriously big browns.

Wooded hills slope back above the lake on the south side, but there's hardly a stick of cover otherwise. This is a perfect lake for float tubes, canoes, or prams, though casting from shore is possible, too, because of the open banks. The best fishing is in the early summer, before the surface layers get too warm, and again in the fall. You can still catch fish in August or September, but the warm water may make the experience a little too stressful for the trout. Martis Creek Reservoir, also sometimes called

Little Truckee River, between Stampede and Boca Reservoirs. There's good fishing in the meadow and, just this once, no other anglers.

Martis Lake, is famous for its blood midges, large insects that are found only in such fertile, alkaline waters. There are actually several different subspecies of this midge, varying in color from claret through orange and ginger to buff, and from size 16 to as large as size 10. There's a fair morning hatch of blood midges, and a more prolific one in the evening. The usual lake insects are also abundant, such as Callibaetis mayflies, damselflies, scuds, and smaller midges, and there's a population of green sunfish for the big fish to eat.

The afternoon is usually very windy here, so the shade of the nearby campground is probably the best place to spend it. In the calm of evening, you can fish an emerger pattern in the film, but if there's a bit of a breeze in either the morning or the evening, the fish will feed on the rising midge pupae a few feet below the surface. Suspending a pupa pattern with a tiny split shot below a buoyant emerger can be very effective. Some fly fishers use an indicator to support the nymph, instead. Watch the ripple pattern carefully for the disturbances caused by a feeding fish, because retrieving a midge pupa across its path will bring a thumping take. Sinking-line techniques work here, as well, even when fishing nymphs. The best way to tempt a really large trout, though, may be with a streamer such as a Zonker.

To get to the lake, take Highway 267 south from Truckee, go past the airport, and turn left at the sign for Martis Creek Reservoir. A paved road leads to the campground, then a dirt road continues down the hill to the lake, where there are several open parking areas. You can launch car-top boats, but motors aren't allowed. The inlet stream and its tributaries are closed to all fishing, and below the dam, much of the creek runs through an ugly gravel-mining operation.

THE LITTLE TRUCKEE RIVER
DeLorme: p. 81, A4–A7
USFS: Tahoe National Forest
USGS: Webber Peak, Independence Lake, Hobart Mills, Boca
Altitude: 6800–5500 feet
Water types: Pools and pocket water, then a meadow stream,
  then riffles and pools.
Trout: Rainbows, 9–17 inches; browns, 10–18 inches, some bigger;
a few brook trout.
Special Regulations: From Stampede to Boca Reservoirs, two
trout, maximum size 14 inches total, only artificial lures with
barbless hooks permitted.

The Little Truckee consists of several very different fisheries. It flows out of Webber Lake (a private, membership-only fishery), then over a falls into a brief, but spectacular limestone canyon. Then it meanders slowly through beautiful, big meadows towered over by snow-covered peaks along Henness Pass Road. In the early summer, wildflowers carpet the meadows, particularly where spring seeps feed into the river. There are some brown trout in this section, but the flow drops so low that they can be tough to catch. It enters a shallow canyon next and picks up a little gradient, so it's a rocky little pool-and-riffle river that flows alongside Highway 89 toward Stampede Reservoir. This stretch gets plenty of bait-fishing pressure from the campgrounds and receives regular infusions of hatchery trout. From Stampede to Boca is different again, a controlled-flow tailwater fishery with picky trout. It flows through an open valley with pine-covered slopes to the west and sagebrush flats to the east, then through a short, rocky section into Boca Reservoir.

I've never tried the river between Webber Lake and the falls, because the flow drops too low to support much of a trout population. Below the falls, it is another matter. It was quite a surprise to find this short, pink-and-yellow limestone canyon, since it's completely hidden from the road. In the early summer, there are some rainbows of appreciable size to be caught in pools and pockets, along with occasional smaller browns and brooks. But by midsummer, most of the flow vanishes under the rocks, and the fish migrate downstream. General fly patterns will work fine in the faster water.

At the head of the meadows, Perazzo Creek joins the Little Truckee and adds a little to the flow. The gradient slows, and it becomes a big meadow stream with undercut banks, the haunt of brown trout and the occasional rainbow. The middle section of these meadows is all private land, but there's similar water on public land just above the diversion dam. This is really an expert's stream, with its open banks and smooth, glassy flows, which drop quite low by the late summer. Terrestrial patterns, including grasshoppers, can lure a large brown or two during the day, and short pieces of faster water may produce the occasional large rainbow, but the evening rise is usually the best time to fish. Mayfly emergers, spent spinners, Little Yellow Stones, and caddis patterns can all bring fish to the surface. Although it's unusual for such smooth water, twitching your fly to attract the browns' attention can work to your advantage here.

The tailwater section from Stampede to Boca Reservoirs is a changing fishery. The uneven flows used to affect it badly, but now the flow regimen has been modified to benefit the trout. There are some really fast-growing fish here, mostly rainbows, with some browns. The Department of Fish and Game planted fingerling rainbows for many years to establish a self-sustaining wild-trout fishery, and it's become a popular venue that sees quite a bit of pressure. The early summer and fall can produce challenging fishing, while midsummer angling can still be a bit of a lottery, since Nevada's demand for water can get the flow ramped up quickly enough to put the hatches off for a while.

This can be truly picky fishing—you might cast to feeding fish for a whole evening and be happy with two fish coming to your fly. It's a very fertile river with a wide variety of mayflies, some of which I've not seen elsewhere, and unlike most tailwaters, they're not all tiny bugs. The Creamy-Orange Dun hatches in early summer (you'll sometimes hear it referred to as a "Sulphur"). Emerger or spinner patterns usually work better than dun patterns, even if you can clearly see that the fish are eating duns. Nymph fishing can cure a case of "What the heck are they eating?" of course, but it can be hard to make yourself do it when every fish in the river is rising. There are some small caddisflies, but unlike on the Truckee, they're less important than the mayflies. In the fall, a run of kokanee salmon enters this section from Boca Reservoir, followed by a few rainbows intent on feeding on their eggs. A yellow marabou streamer will catch you a kokanee if you want to see what one looks like, but don't expect much of a fight.

To reach the upper sections, turn left onto the paved Henness Pass Road from Highway 89. After 5 miles, turn left to Perazzo Meadows, keep straight across at the four-way junction, and you'll come to a bridge over the Little Truckee. The limestone canyon and the falls are upstream to your right. If you turn left at the four-way junction, you'll come to another bridge over the river, and you can fish downstream from there through the meadows. If you turn left off Henness Pass Road 1.0 miles from Highway 89, to Independence Lake, you'll cross the river, then turn right in 0.5 miles. Turn right again on a dirt track in another 0.5 miles and it will lead you down to a parking area above the diversion dam. You can fish upstream through meadows and a short canyon for about half a mile before you enter private land. To reach the section below Stampede, exit Interstate 80 to Boca and head north on Stampede Meadows Road. You'll pass Boca Reservoir, then Boyington Mill Campground. There are several pullouts on the left, from which you walk across sagebrush flats to the river.

PERAZZO CREEK
DeLorme: p. 81, A4/5
USFS: Tahoe National Forest
USGS: Webber Lake
Altitude: 7600–6600 feet
Water types: Small pools and runs, then it becomes
 a meadow stream.
Trout: Browns, 8–12 inches; brook trout, 6–9 inches.

Down in the meadows where it joins the Little Truckee, Perazzo Creek is a meadow stream, degraded by cattle and with little cover for fish. Above

Independence Creek, below the lake. Pocket water with brown trout is an unusual combination.

the meadow, it runs a little faster, among angular blue-gray rocks. Past Department of Fish and Game surveys have turned up good numbers of trout, but when I fished it, a large family of mergansers had taken up residence, so most of the trout I saw were half-eaten. I suspect that the best fishing is farther upstream, where the gradient is steeper.

To get to Perazzo Creek, turn left off Henness Pass Road after 5 miles, cross the Little Truckee, and continue as far as you wish on the dirt road. The stream is to your left.

COLD STREAM
DeLorme: p. 81, A5
USFS: Tahoe National Forest
USGS: Webber Peak
Altitude: 8200–6500 feet
Water types: A tiny meadow stream that then turns into little
   pools and runs.
Trout: Brook trout, 5–9 inches, plus some browns.

In 1997, the spring floods really did a number on the lower reaches of this stream, washing all the trout into the Little Truckee. Far upstream, though, is a beautiful high alpine meadow, dotted with gentians and other wildflowers and laced by the broad curves of a tiny meadow stream full of equally tiny brook trout. Just below this, the gradient steepens a little, and the miniature pools and runs hide some slightly larger brookies, while there are still small meadows and wildflowers to admire. This would be a nice getaway for the beginner frustrated by the Little Truckee.

To get there, turn left off Henness Pass Road 1 mile from Highway 89, to Independence Lake, then right in 0.5 miles. You're now on a dirt road that parallels Henness Pass Road on the other side of the Little Truckee. Turn left in 3.5 miles, stay right at the top of the hill at the only junction, and you'll drop down and cross Cold Stream after 3 miles, coming to the meadow in another half-mile. Note: this logging road appears only on the topo map and is not for passenger cars.

INDEPENDENCE CREEK
DeLorme: p. 81, A5
USFS: Tahoe National Forest
USGS: Independence Lake
Altitude: 7000–6300 feet
Water types: Small pools, runs, and pocket water.
Trout: Browns, 9–12 inches; rainbows, 7–10 inches.

Independence Creek is relatively unusual for a small stream in that its flow is controlled by a dam. The tailwater outflow from Independence Lake increases the creek's fertility. This is reflected in a strong population of brown trout that grow fairly large. The creek exits the lake in an artificially straightened channel, then, just above the first road crossing, it becomes a plunge-pool and pocket-water stream, rather closely hemmed in by alder bushes. This section might not be ideal for beginners, but a mile downstream, the terrain opens up a little, and small meadows border the stream, while some log and tree-root cover shelters fish. Down there, rainbows are as plentiful as browns, and some of them grow fairly large, as well. Independence Creek contains both caddisflies and mayflies, but a general pattern like the Adams is quite sufficient.

To get there, turn left off Henness Pass Road in 1 mile from Highway 89, to Independence Lake, then go straight across at the first cross-roads. At the next crossroads, a left turn will bring you down to the stream. If you continue straight across, the dirt road parallels the stream, but there usually are washouts where two small streams cross, so following the stream in a passenger car isn't recommended. You can hike in anywhere along here. Then the road bends away from the stream a little as it nears the lake. If you take the first left turn, it will bring you back to a bridge over Independence Creek. You can fish downstream from there. If you were to continue on this road, it eventually would lead to Sagehen Creek. Note that Independence Creek above Independence Lake is closed to all fishing.

SAGEHEN CREEK

DeLorme: p. 81, A5–A6
USFS: Tahoe National Forest
USGS: Independence Lake, Hobart Mills
Altitude: 7000–5800 feet
Water types: A little meadow stream with undercuts and logs, pools and runs.
Trout: Browns, 8–12 inches; rainbows, 7–11 inches; brook trout, 6–9 inches.
Special Regulations: From the Highway 89 bridge to the gauging station, fishing is catch-and-release only, limited to artificial lures and barbless hooks. Fishing is prohibited upstream of the gauging station for 1/2 mile.

Sagehen Creek runs through a long, shallow valley from which springs bubble up and provide most of the flow. Up at Sagehen Campground is a pretty meadow where the stream and the trout are both quite small. Then the valley closes in a little by the University of California Research Station. Between the gauging station and the highway, it meanders through flower-filled meadows where undercut banks provide cover. Below the bridge, its gradient increases and it flows into a shallow, U-shaped canyon where lodgepole pines grow in a meadow and provide log cover when they fall. Then the valley opens up again as the stream nears Stampede Reservoir.

Up at the campground, you'll find brook trout and native rainbows, but as I said, the fish are as tiny as the creek. Fishing is actually a bit better in the tangles of brush well upstream from the campground. Down where Highway 89 crosses Sagehen Creek, there are brown trout in the narrow meadows above and below the bridge. The special-regulations section, upstream of Highway 89, offers challenging fishing. Undercuts can hide some sizable browns, but there's little broken water or rock cover to make trout feel secure. For that reason, the less experienced fly fisher should head downstream, where the water flows a little faster and the fishing is a little easier, though the trout may be smaller. The stream has very substantial populations of mayflies and caddisflies, but it's so tiny that the hatches are sparse and varied, and the trout aren't selective. A general pattern really does seem to work best, such as an Elk Hair Caddis or yes, the Adams again. Surprisingly for a stream surrounded by meadows, terrestrial patterns don't seem to be particularly successful, at least in my experience.

Getting there is easy. Park at the Highway 89 bridge and fish up or down (there's a good trail on the north bank downstream). To access farther upstream, continue north past the bridge for about half a mile, then turn left on the dirt road signposted to Sagehen Campground. You soon come to a four-way junction. Left is a closed-off dirt road that leads down to the creek. Straight across is a gated road you can hike to get upstream to the research station. It runs parallel to, but well above the creek. If you turn right, Sagehen Campground is 4 miles. To get there this way, next turn left in 1 mile (Independence Lake is straight on), then turn left at a T junction in another 2.5 miles. If you turn right at the T junction, the road will take you upstream, broadly parallel to the creek.

PROSSER CREEK
DeLorme: p. 81, A/B5–6
USFS: Tahoe National Forest
USGS: Independence Lake, Hobart Mills
Altitude: 7500–5700 feet
Water types: Small pools and runs, some pocket water.
Trout: Rainbows, 7–12 inches; browns, 9–12 inches; brook trout, 7–9 inches.

You'll see plenty of cars and trucks parked where the highway crosses Prosser Creek. The Department of Fish and Game graces it with the most planters of any stream in the area, so those vehicles usually belong to bait fishers and spin anglers. Head upstream, though, and you'll find good numbers of wild trout. Prosser Creek's two forks join just west of Prosser Hill. The South Fork starts as several tiny streams that join in fertile meadows on private land, and it then flows through a short, brush-filled canyon. The North Fork is about twice the South Fork's size and flows through a long, fairly deep valley, most of which is also private land.

I haven't hiked to the upper reaches of the North Fork, above the private land, but I suspect it would be well worthwhile. The lower reaches of both streams and the main stem below the fork offer some pretty enjoy-

Sagehen Creek, downstream from Highway 89. This stream provides a challenge for small-water enthusiasts.

able fishing. Rainbows are the principal trout of the North Fork and main stem, while the South Fork contains brook trout, some rainbows, and a few sizable browns. The North Fork is the more open of the two, with more pocket water and lots of small rainbows, so it's probably the better fishery for the beginner. Both are fertile, with abundant populations of mayflies and caddisflies, and capable of producing quite large trout for a small stream.

To get to the upper reaches of Prosser Creek from Truckee, take Highway 89 north, then turn left onto Alder Creek Road. Turn right onto a dirt road in 2.7 miles, then it's 1.2 miles to the bridge over the South Fork. The road continues into the valley of the North Fork, but it's mostly private land, though a trail parallels the stream from the end of the dirt road. The forks are just downstream of the bridge.

ALDER CREEK
DeLorme: p. 71, B5–6
USFS: Tahoe National Forest
USGS: Norden, Truckee
Altitude: 7200–5700 feet
Water types: A wooded meadow stream with tiny pools and
log structure.
Trout: Rainbows, 6–10 inches; browns, 6–8 inches; brook trout,
6–9 inches.

Alder Creek is a really tiny stream, but it does offer some early-season fishing close to Truckee. It's completely hidden in a brush-choked gully through the Tahoe-Donner residential area, but it opens up a little past Alder Creek Campground. Below there, the new Emigrant Heritage Trail runs along it for more than 2 miles. It's very pretty, with plenty of wildflowers, and the fishing is pleasantly challenging, though the dense brush would tax beginners. Below Highway 89, it runs through an open meadow, then divides into tiny channels just before it flows into Prosser Creek Reservoir. The trout are mainly rainbows, with a few baby browns, and with brookies in the upper reaches. To get there, turn left off Highway 89 onto Alder Creek Road, which parallels the creek.

LAKE OF THE WOODS
DeLorme: p. 71, D5
USFS: Tahoe National Forest
USGS: Truckee
Altitude: 7400 feet
Trout: Planted browns.

Lake of the Woods is a small, pretty lake completely surrounded by woods, and it sees a lot of fishing pressure because of the many campsites available—it's a popular spot. When I researched it, it contained a population of wild browns, fish that were rescued from Milton Reservoir when it was drained for repairs. This is going to be a temporary situation, though, because the lake has no inflow stream, the outflow dries up by early summer, and brown trout are fall, in-stream spawners. However, the Department of Fish and Game plants it with fingerling browns, and it's fertile enough for them to get big—I saw them jumping for dragonflies like bass. There were huge numbers of damselflies, too, so a damsel nymph is a good pattern. You'll need a float tube to fish here.

To get to Lake of the Woods, take the first right turn off Henness Pass Road 5.5 miles from Highway 89. It's signposted to Lake of the Woods. The dirt road forks in 1.5 miles, but both choices lead to the lake.

INDEPENDENCE LAKE
DeLorme: p. 81, A5
USFS: Tahoe National Forest
USGS: Truckee
Altitude: 7000 feet
Trout: Wild browns, brook trout, Lahontan cutthroats, and whitefish.
Special Regulations: Artificial lures and flies only. Catch-and-release only for cutthroat trout, and a limit of five for any other trout. The tributaries and the lake within 300 feet of them are closed to fishing.

Independence Lake is a very large body of water that was once two natural lakes. It sits in a long valley, with slopes clad in fir and pines on either side. Because it runs from southwest to northeast, the prevailing winds blow straight down its length, which means that even in a comparatively gentle breeze, there's a pronounced swell down at the dam end. This doesn't make it ideal for the float tuber, but for the fly fisher who's lucky enough to own a small boat, it could be a great lake to fish.

This lake is a precious resource, because it has the only pure strain of native Lahontan cutthroats adapted to living in a lake system. For some reason, these trout didn't interbreed with the various strains of rainbows that were planted there in the past, so it supplies pure-strain cutthroats for the breeding program at Heenan Lake, among other places. It also has a few wild browns, some sizeable brook trout, and the unusual bonus of lots of whitefish, not something you can catch in many lakes in California. Though I can't say how big the trout get for sure, it contains lots of crayfish, a prime big-trout food. Much of the lake bed is medium-sized cobble, which is unusual, and with oxygenation from the constant wave action, this supports an extraordinary variety of insect life. I've seen Mahogany Duns, Blue-Winged Olive mayflies, and medium-sized olive stoneflies, all of which are normally river insects, among the more usual caddisflies and midges.

To get there from Truckee, turn left off Highway 89 to Sagehen Campground, turn right at the first junction, then stay straight on when another turn presents itself in a mile, following the sign to the lake. You will need a high-clearance vehicle for this dirt road. You can also get here from Henness Pass Road, but again, you'll need a high-clearance vehicle, and preferably four-wheel drive, too. (See the Independence Creek listing above for directions.)

LODGING IN TRUCKEE

Alpine Village Motel
On Deerfield Road
1-800-933-1787

Donner Lake Village Resort
Hotel On Donner Pass Road
(530) 587-6081

Loch Leven Lodge
On Donner Pass Road
(530) 587-3773

Richardson House
Bed and breakfast, on High Street
(530) 587-5833

Star Hotel
On West River Street
(530) 587-3007

Super 8 Lodge
On Highway 267
1-800-800-8000

Truckee Tahoe Inn (Best Western)
On Highway 267
1-800-824-6385

Truckee Hotel
A period hotel on High Street
(530) 587-4444

CAMPING IN THE TRUCKEE AREA

All are National Forest Service campgrounds unless otherwise stated. Those that charge a fee are operated by concessionaires and cost an average of $10 per site. Sites at those marked with the telephone symbol ☎ can be reserved by calling 1-800-280-CAMP. There is no undeveloped camping in the Truckee area. The only place to find any is in the Little Truckee drainage, off Henness Pass Road, but only by a long drive on the dirt roads that lead off the pavement.

Granite Flat
Highway 89 South
Fee, piped water

Goose Meadows ☎
Highway 89 South
Fee, hand pumped water

Silver Creek ☎
Highway 89 South
Fee, hand pumped water

Alder Creek
Alder Creek Road
Private campground,
hot showers, reasonable fee

Lakeside
Prosser Reservoir
Fee, piped water

Prosser
Prosser Reservoir
Fee, piped water

Sagehen
Off Highway 89
No fee, no water

Little Truckee Lower ☎
Highway 89
Fee, piped water

Little Truckee Upper ☎
Highway 89
Fee, piped water

Independence Lake
Off Highway 89
Private campground,
fee, piped water

Logger Campground ☎
Stampede Reservoir
Fee, piped water

Davies Creek Campground
Stampede Reservoir
No fee, no water

Boyington Mill
Boca Reservoir
Fee, no water

Boca Rest
Boca Reservoir
Fee, piped water

Boca
Boca Reservoir
Fee, no water

Boca Spring
Boca Reservoir
Fee, unimproved camp, spring water
(Note that this last campground lacks picnic tables, but does have plenty of shade, unlike the previous three, which can bake in the sun)

Fly-Fishing Supplies

Mountain Hardware and Sports
11320 Donner Pass Road
Truckee, CA 96160
(530) 587-4844
A selection of flies, fly-fishing, and camping equipment.

Truckee River Outfitters
10200 Donner Pass Road
Truckee, CA 96161
(530) 582-0900
A full-service fly shop, opened in 1998.

Other Supplies

Groceries and camping supplies are available in Truckee. There's a Safeway in the Gateway Shopping Center. Exit Interstate 80 to 89 South, but go north to the shopping center. You can fill propane tanks at the Sierra Super-Stop gas station on the south side of Donner Pass Road heading out of Truckee toward Safeway and Mountain Hardware.

Chapter 6: The Yuba River Area

Picture this: hillsides are transformed into torrents of mud and gravel as gold miners hose away the earth with gigantic high-pressure jets of water. The complete course of a river is diverted to gain access to gold-bearing rock. Rude camps of tents and shacks appear almost overnight, then vanish just as quickly, once a deep-rock vein is tapped out. Thousands of men live on little more than hardtack and hard liquor, so starved for the company of women that when one arrives in town, most of the male citizens turn out to escort her down muddy Main Street. The rule of law struggles against claim jumping, robbery, murder, and frontier justice in the form of lynchings. A few men know the heady excitement of striking it rich, but most just feel the bitter despair of hard labor and sixteen-hour days that generate nothing but empty pockets and spent lives.

North Fork of the Yuba River, downstream from Highway 49. Good water for early and late season angling.

All of these things occurred along the forks of the Yuba River and their tributaries during the latter half of the nineteenth century, when the region was a hotbed of gold-mining activity. Today, little remains of the once-flourishing miners' camps but names on maps and piles of rock along the streams. The towns where these men gambled and drank and paid fabulous prices for food and supplies are now just quiet communities of families and retirees, if they exist at all. A small number of hobbyists still dredge for "color" in the area's streams, but those who walk the banks are more likely to be seeking fish than fortune. The Yuba River drainage offers all kinds of angling opportunities—riches, in a way—for fly fishers in search of wild trout and challenging fishing.

THE NORTH FORK OF THE YUBA RIVER

DeLorme: p. 70, D3; p. 69, D6
USFS: Tahoe National Forest
USGS: Haypress Valley, Sierra City, Downieville, Goodyears Bar
Altitude: 7000–2200 feet
Water types: From beaver ponds through small pools, runs,
and pocket water to large pools and riffles.
Trout: Rainbows, 9–17 inches; browns, 9–24 inches; brook trout,
7–10 inches in the headwaters.
Special: From the western boundary of Sierra City to Ladies Canyon
Creek, two trout, minimum size 10 inches, only artificial lures with
barbless hooks permitted.

The North Fork is not only the most significant branch of the Yuba River, but also the most accessible, since Highway 49 parallels most of its length. It starts at the very crest of the Sierra as two tiny, spring-fed creeks that converge in a small alpine meadow beneath Yuba Pass. This meadow is dotted in season with the blue of lupines and delphiniums, the red of Indian paintbrush, and the white of bog-candle orchids and marsh marigolds, all sustained by water from long-established beaver ponds. The North Fork exits the beaver ponds as a small stream, burbling through shallow pools among alder bushes for several miles before bursting into the top of a steeply falling, rocky canyon below Bassett's. Salmon Creek substantially increases its flow there, and it's further augmented at Big Springs, where a group of springs bubble out of the side of the canyon and flow under Highway 49. You can see them at the back of a

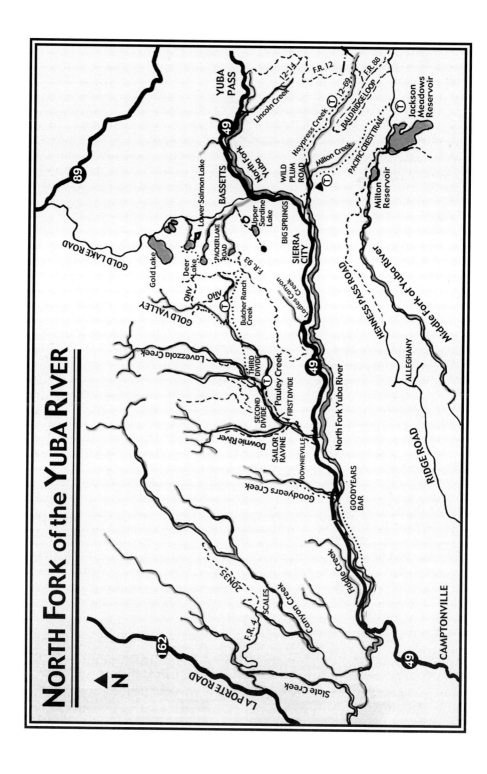

big pullout on the northwest side of the highway.

The North Fork then cuts through a narrow slot in solid bedrock and tumbles over Loves Falls. Just above Sierra City, Haypress Creek adds another 50 percent to the flow, and it is here that the North Fork of the Yuba takes on the characteristics of a true river, pushing through deep pools and heavy pocket water for the 11 miles to Downieville. The river is far below the road downstream of Downieville, most of the way to Goodyears Bar. The elevation changes less steeply, so it becomes more of a pool-and-riffle river running through a broad flood plain. These conditions continue, with the river running adjacent to the highway, all the way to the bridge where Highway 49 crosses the river and starts to climb southward, toward Grass Valley. The river continues through a narrower canyon, accessible only by hiking trails, to Bullard's Bar Reservoir. This impoundment swallows the river whole and spits it out through the Colgate Tunnel into Englebright Lake.

In the headwaters, you'll find small brookies in the beaver ponds, together with a unique, deeply colored strain of rainbows with larger, leopardlike spots and a narrow, deep-red stripe with a little yellow beneath it. They have parr marks, even when fully grown, and a distinctive white edge on their anal fins. In the small stream below the ponds, brown trout start to appear, hiding in the small undercuts in the meadow and beneath bushes and next to large rocks in the shallow pools and runs farther down. This section, down to about Chapman Creek, gives the fly fisher the chance to catch all three species of trout, though few will be over 10 inches.

As you approach Bassett's, a more silvery strain of rainbow takes over the stream, and these are the predominant trout throughout the rest of the river. From Sierra City downstream, they average 10 to 12 inches, with fish of 14 to 16 inches quite common. Brown trout are present throughout, some of them very large fish, but they appear to be heavily outnumbered by the rainbows. It's generally accepted that most of the larger browns are migratory fish from Bullard's Bar Reservoir.

The lower river, below the Highway 49 bridge, hosts runs of rainbows in the spring, but is best fished in the fall, when the flows are lower than they are in the spring and the water has cooled from its midsummer highs. Department of Fish and Game surveys in 1992 showed that there were almost four thousand trout per mile, 80 percent of them rainbows. Angler returns from the Wild Trout section from 1993 to 1996 showed a catch rate between one and one and a half trout per hour, almost 90 percent rainbows.

All fly-fishing methods will work on the North Fork. Nymphing with an indicator is very successful in pocket water and riffles, but so is fishing attractor dry flies, size 10 to size 14. Try Wulffs, Trudes, or Humpies, depending on which you find in your box. The keen hatch matcher can concentrate on the pools and find rising fish at some time of the day all season long. Traditional wet-fly fishing also will catch fish early in the season and again on summer evenings when caddisflies hatch. The main hatches are tabulated below, but it should be stressed that there's such a variety of aquatic insects that general patterns usually work just as well as specific imitations. The trout might have the choice of several mayflies emerging at the same time, but they're probably not going to be selective. Nymph fishers also will find their own favorite patterns to be just as effective as anything I might recommend, since in the North Fork's swirling currents, the trout are opportunists. But if you really need advice, I'd take a Bird's Nest in size 12 to size 16 against all comers.

One of the best hatches on the river is a creamy-orange mayfly, about a size 16, that emerges in very good numbers on early summer evenings. This insect is very important throughout the Yuba system, and it's also found on the Truckee, where Ralph Cutter has identified it as *Ephemerella Tibialis,* now reclassified as *Serratella Tibialis,* for those who need to know the Latin name. This makes a Light Cahill a good general pattern, and a creamy-orange Sparkle Dun even more useful. Rusty-colored mayfly spinners from size 14 to size 18 fall on summer evenings, joining a parade of various small, pale-colored duns just as the caddises start to hatch, too. Golden Stoneflies are common in the early summer, so carry some size 8 Stimulators and Golden Stone nymphs. The October Caddis hatch may be eagerly awaited, but as on many other rivers, it's elusive, failing to appear at all on many days. You'll encounter the greatest concentrations of these large, orange-bodied caddisflies in the upper part of the special-regulations section, but be aware that the water is very cold by then, so fishing can be slow if they fail to show. The *Baetis* or Blue-Winged Olive hatch is a fairly sparse event on the upper river, but it's good enough lower down to offer the chance of catching large rainbows on small dries, particularly below the Highway 49 bridge. The hatch starts late there, as late as 3:00 P.M., and lasts for about two hours. A size 18 Sparkle Dun is a good imitation. And there are always midges on cool mornings and early in the evenings.

NORTH FORK OF THE YUBA HATCH TABLE

Insect	Dates	Size
Creamy-Orange Dun (Serratella aka Ephemerella Tibialis)	mid June–August	16
Pale Evening Duns (various)	July–September	18–22
Blue-Winged Olive (Baetis)	mid-September–November	18–20
Green Sedge (Rhyacophila)	May–September	10–14
Spotted Sedge (Hydrophsyche)	mid-May–September	12–14
Saddle-Case Caddis (Glossosoma)	June–July	16
October Caddis (Dicosmoecus)	October–November	6–8
Golden Stonefly (Calineuria)	May–mid-July	6–10
Midges	All season	20–24

This hatch table is equally valid for the South Fork of the Yuba. The Middle Fork lacks the larger insects, while the smallest ones are very abundant because it's an artificially enriched tailwater, with low flows nearly all year.

As you've already gathered, the highway offers easy access to most of the river. There are some stretches, though, where access may be across private land, and it is helpful to refer to the mileage markers that Caltrans erects to help them find things that need maintaining, such as bridges and drainage gullies. The first access is where Highway 49 crosses the bridge at the 3.70 mile marker. If you pull out on the north side, you can access the river downstream. A gravel road behind a locked barrier on the northwest side (marked with a brown sign for Canyon Creek Trailhead) leads a mile to Shenanigan Flat, a former campground that's now a miners' encampment. The water offers good fishing opportunities both upstream and downstream, better than back at the bridge. Fishing is best in the fall, when the water has cooled down and the miners have stopped dredging. The dirt road continues another mile to Cherokee Creek, a very steep hundred feet above the river, and there are only two miners' trails leading down. Below Cherokee Creek, a formal trail continues another mile and a half to the junction with Canyon Creek. There are some big pools down there that can produce some rainbows of decent size during hatches, but don't be fooled by the suckers and hardheads that cruise the depths and do a poor imitation of big browns.

There are innumerable accesses from the bridge upstream to Goodyears Bar at the 12.30 mile marker, including six campgrounds. This means planted fish and plenty of fishing pressure throughout this section. Even so, numbers of wild fish can still be caught, particularly during the evening rise. The fishing from Fiddle Creek up to Indian Valley Campground (at the 5.35 mile marker) is particularly good. If you want to get away from the crowds, you should know that the Yuba River Trail runs along the south side of the river for 7 miles, starting at Rocky Rest Campground (the 5.70 mile marker), where a footbridge crosses the river, and ending at Goodyears Bar. If you want a shady parking spot at the other end, turn right to Goodyears Bar off Highway 49, cross the river, and turn right at the T junction. You will cross two tiny creeks, then you'll see the trail sign pointing uphill to your right and the parking spot on your left. The trail is often high above the river, but subsidiary trails lead down. Back on the main road at the 11.36 mile marker, there's a good miners' trail down to the river and some enjoyable fishing water.

Upstream from Goodyears Bar, the river is wide open and shallow until the next good access, at the 14.64 mile marker, where a track runs down to the river behind a locked barrier. From here to Downieville, the river is a little away from the highway and the fishing's pretty good. From Downieville, you can also cross the bridge to the south side of the river and fish back downstream. I haven't spent much time on the 7-mile stretch from Downieville upstream to Ladies Canyon Creek, since the river is often uncomfortably close to the highway. Pullouts are frequent, though, and the fishing can be just as good as on the Wild Trout section, where fly fishers tend to concentrate. This starts at Ladies Canyon Creek (at the 24.80 mile marker) and runs to the western boundary of Sierra City. The river is soon well below the highway, and accesses are fewer. Just past Fournier Ranch (the 26.00 mile marker) there's a pullout on the right. An old miners' trail goes round the point of the bluff, and if you take it to the left, you'll find a steep trail down. At Shannon's Cabins, (the 27.30 mile marker), you can pull off to the right on a dirt track and keep left to a parking area. (Don't block the road behind the locked gate on the right, which leads to a mining claim.) A trail leads down to the river and some good pool and pocket water. Upstream, you'll find a deep whirlpool below the remains of the Gillespie Dam, a demented attempt to divert the river for some mining purpose. At Loganville Campground (the 27.70 mile marker), you can park off the road and walk through to the river. The final access to the Wild Trout section is down a track to the left of Herrington's Resort at the 28.80 mile marker.

Through Sierra City to Haypress Creek, the water is much the same as it is in the Wild Trout section, but you will run into planted fish and some bait-fishing pressure on the weekends. Above the bridge at Wild Plum Road (at the 29.90 mile marker), you'll find steeply falling pool-and-pocket water that provides angling for rainbows to 12 inches. The narrower sections around Loves Falls are tough to fish, but can be accessed by walking the Pacific Crest Trail, which crosses the highway at the 31.20 mile marker, down to the river. Access is pretty easy from Bassett's upstream, since the much smaller stream is usually quite close to the highway. The fish may be small, but the surroundings are lovely, as tiny meadows and wildflowers alternate with the dense alders and log structure. The beaver ponds at the top can be reached by parking in a pull-out at the 40.22 mile marker and walking back down a diagonal track into the meadow.

LINCOLN CREEK
DeLorme: p. 70, C/D3
USFS: Tahoe National Forest
USGS: Haypress Valley
Altitude: 7000–6200 feet
Water types: A tiny meadow stream, then little pools and pocket water.
Trout: Rainbows; 7–10 inches; browns, 8–11 inches.

Tiny Lincoln Creek rises from springs in a small valley, then meanders through a large, open meadow that was once a lake. Years ago, the stream washed out the natural dam at the mouth and cut a narrow course through the old lake bed. Below the meadow, it falls swiftly through a shallow, V-shaped canyon to its junction with the North Yuba. Irregularly shaped gray-and-gold boulders create tiny pools and pocket water, though brushy alders make it very tough to fish in many places.

Lincoln Creek contains the strain of beautiful, wild rainbows found in the North Yuba headwaters, and it's also the only tributary that has a significant brown trout population. In the top meadow, it's necessary to cast across land to the spooky little rainbows, so that only the dry fly and tippet land in the yard-wide stream. Though it might be fun, this marshy meadow should be approached only with the greatest caution before fall, since it may be the single most mosquito-infested spot in the Sierra Nevada. In the canyon below, you'll find slightly larger rainbows, and more brown trout the closer you get to the Yuba. Many of the pools are quite shallow, but the angular rocks and overhanging alders provide cover, and insects are abundant.

To reach the top meadow, turn right off Highway 49 on Yuba Pass Road (Forest Road 12). Drive 4.2 miles to the second turning on the right, signposted to Lincoln Valley (Forest Road 12-14). The road dead-ends at the far end of the meadow, and you can fish up, but only if basted thoroughly from a gallon vat of insect repellent. To reach the lower section, turn right off Highway 49 at the 38.78 mile marker. Walk round the barrier with the "Road Closed" sign on it and ford the shallow North Yuba. A bridge here once led to a campground, but it washed out and never was replaced. Hike the gravel road on the far side and in seven minutes you'll come to a spur on the left leading to another washed-out bridge over Lincoln Creek. If you stay on the road, then fork left on a logging spur in a few hundred yards, you can walk upstream for half a mile, crossing a tiny stream, before the track peters out close to the creek.

SALMON CREEK
DeLorme: p. 70, C/D2
USFS: Tahoe National Forest
USGS: Haypress Valley
Altitude: 5700–5200 feet
Water types: Little rocky pools and pocket water.
Trout: Rainbows, 7–10 inches

Salmon Creek collects the outflow from much of the Lakes Basin area and smashes down its steep valley in the spring, so you have to clamber through a broad boulder field to fish it. Eager, small rainbows can make that worthwhile until the flow drops in late summer. After that, larger fish are far outnumbered by tiny juveniles, so this must be a spawning stream for the main river. It's wide-open for casting room, so it's recommended for the beginner, but it might be tough going for the elderly.

To reach it, turn left off Highway 49 just before the bridge over Salmon Creek and park there, rather than driving up this private road. Packer Lake Road crosses the creek farther up, but above the bridge, the stream runs through a campground where it is very heavily planted and fished, and above its junction with Packer Creek there is very little flow.

HAYPRESS CREEK
DeLorme: p. 70, D4–D3
USFS: Tahoe National Forest
USGS: Haypress Valley
Altitude: 6600–4300 feet
Water types: A little meadow stream, then pools and pocket water.
Trout: Rainbows, 8–12 inches; brook trout, 6–10 inches.

Haypress Creek is a prolific stream with varied scenery and equally varied fishing. It begins as a narrow, willow-edged brook surrounded by wildflowers and boggy little springs in a hidden meadow in the high country between the Middle and North Forks of the Yuba. Then it meanders through the slow pools of a second meadow into a shallow, brushy canyon. After a couple of miles, it increases in gradient and becomes a rocky plunge-pool stream for the last third of its journey to the North Yuba, slowing down only in the flood-ravaged pools by Wild Plum Campground.

In the meadows at the top, brook trout reign. They're mostly little buccaneers from 6 to 8 inches, but the granddaddies may go 10. Any tiny dry fly will catch them, since they mostly subsist on midges. As you go down into the canyon, the small, deep pools will contain a few brookies, but the long, shallow ones are a better bet for fish. You can have a fifty-fish day here, and you could happily take a few for the pan, since they've overpopulated. Roughly half a mile below Long Valley Creek there is a six-foot falls, below which the brookies will be fewer and skinnier. Now the center of every pool will hold plump, silvery rainbows, which sometimes reach 12 inches. You can use a slightly larger dry fly here, since the insect life includes the more sizable mayflies, caddisflies, and stoneflies found in a typical freestone stream. If you access Haypress Creek from

Milton Creek, close to the Pacific Crest Trail. Beautiful little wild rainbows can be found in the shade beneath the alders.

the lower end, it falls steeply through a mass of gray boulders flung down by spring floods, with little good holding water, and the fish population is lower as a result. Near the campground at the bottom, you will catch the occasional planted rainbow. Haypress Creek's two main tributaries are Long Valley Creek, which is tiny and almost unfishable because of thick brush, but which does hold some brookies, and Milton Creek, which is a pleasant fishery, dealt with below.

You can reach Haypress Creek from several directions. The meadow at the top can be reached by taking Henness Pass Road off Highway 89 north from Truckee. Take the first turnoff signposted to Forest Road 88 (the Bald Ridge Loop) on the right after Webber Lake, not the second turnoff so posted. This is a good dirt road that goes over the hill and drops down toward the top meadow. In about 2 miles, stay right where Forest Road 88 heads left and you'll cross Haypress Creek on a railroad trestle bridge. After the bridge, keep left, and you'll come to the second meadow in 1.5 miles. Park at the earth barrier in 0.5 miles, then hike the closed-off jeep road downstream. If you stay left back at that first junction on the Bald Ridge Loop, you can access the middle stretch of the creek after 4.0 miles by parking in a pullout and hiking down the hill a short way.

You should be just below a tiny tributary that enters from the south, the direction from which you approach. Notice that for some distance before this, a steep ridge rises between the road and the creek and prevents access. You must carry a topo map to accomplish this short cross-country hike. If you keep going for another 0.6 miles, you'll come to a gravel road that goes 1.0 miles down to a new hydropower dam. (I recommend walking this, since fallen trees often block the road.) Turn right, down into the canyon, in about 0.7 miles.

To reach the bottom end of Haypress Creek from Highway 49, turn right on Wild Plum Road, just east of Sierra City at the 29.9 mile marker. Then follow the signs to Wild Plum Campground, crossing the bridge over the North Yuba. Park in the trailhead parking area on the right before the campground, from which a steeply climbing trail goes upstream. If you want to access the upper reaches from Highway 49, drive up to Yuba Pass, then turn right on Forest Road 12, following it for 10.8 miles to a turning on the right, signposted "Haypress Valley 3 miles." (This is Forest Road 12–69.) In about a mile, turn left into the top meadow or continue straight on to the second meadow and the north-side trail.

MILTON CREEK
DeLorme: p. 70, D3
USFS: Tahoe National Forest
USGS: Haypress Valley
Altitude: 5600–4800 feet
Water types: Tiny pools and runs.
Trout: Rainbows, 7–10 inches.

For all I know, the valley through which Milton Creek flows may be young geologically, but it doesn't suffer from the heavy snowmelt that smashes the middle reaches of Haypress Creek into a boulder field, so it feels as if it has always been the way you see it: a stable channel of gray rocks covered in moss, framed by stately trees, with ferns and Indian rhubarb beneath. Milton Creek can make you understand how those over-used cathedral metaphors get applied to streams. The bankside alders and poplars stand as straight as columns, while boughs of dogwood and maple form a vaulted ceiling above. The fall colors are quite a sight.

Close to its junction with Haypress Creek, Milton Creek slows into broad, shallow pools, so the best fishing is a short hike up the Pacific Crest Trail. The rainbows are pretty, delicately colored, if not big, and quite abun-

Downie River, upstream from the mining camps. A hiking trail takes you to good fishing in wild country.

dant. The red stripe is faint, with a hint of gold beneath and a sheen from violet to green above that gleams in the dappled light beneath the tree canopy. The trout hold in the deeper slots at the tail of the tiny pools, so you should approach each one carefully and take your time. Admire the surroundings first, then think about where the fish might be before you cast. This stream presents a true challenge for a small-stream enthusiast, but may not be the best place for a beginner, since the vegetation hems it in rather closely.

To get to Milton Creek, start from Wild Plum Road, off Highway 49. (See the Haypress Creek listing above.) Park in the trailhead parking area and hike through the campground to the west end of the upper loop. Continue uphill on the gravel road, which goes almost a mile before the Pacific Crest Trail crosses it. Turn right onto the trail and follow it upstream, or continue a few yards to a bridge over Milton Creek. If you take the PCT, you'll come to a new hydro dam in three-quarters of a mile, an absurd anachronism in this pristine environment. But above this excrescence, all is calm, all is bright.

THE DOWNIE RIVER

DeLorme: p. 70, C1–D1
USFS: Tahoe National Forest
USGS: Mt. Fillmore, Downieville
Altitude: 4000–3000 feet
Water types: Pools, runs, and pocket water.
Trout: Rainbows, 6–11 inches, plus occasional browns.

The Downie River is named for Major William Downie and joins the North Yuba at the historic Gold Rush town of Downieville, which it doesn't take genius to deduce is also named for the good major. It is one of three streams that join within the limits of Downieville, the others being Pauley and Lavezzola Creeks, also named after respected former citizens. The main stem is then named the Downie "River," despite the fact that both Lavezzola and Pauley Creeks carry at least as much water. You will see the junction of the Downie and the North Yuba if you glance back just after you pass through town on Highway 49. All three streams have cut deep canyons, so they fall less steeply than most North Yuba tributaries. They also seem to be spring-fed, and Lavezzola and Pauley Creeks are very fertile, while the Downie is slightly less so. Together, they offer some of the finest small-stream fishing in the Sierra.

The Downie River starts due north of town, formed by the junction of numerous small streams, then flows through a narrow canyon composed of gray slate. Often the stream runs in a U-shaped trough in the slate with no cover of gravel or rocks, so it looks like a natural swimming pool with a blue-gray bottom and "lanes" delineated by veins of white quartz. Small springs percolate out of the canyon wall into tiny, bowl-shaped pools surrounded by ferns and mosses, then spill into the stream. This lovely section is reached only by the Downie River Trail. Lower down, the canyon is a little broader and fully inhabited by gold miners. In places, you'll spot the ruins of old miners' cabins and even the abandoned orchard that someone once planted, red and black plums hanging incongruously in a thicket of berry bushes and creeping vines. Here the stream has more rocky pockets and runs, while many of the pools are artificially altered by all the suction dredging. Most of the rainbows are small, but they're so abundant that this is a good place for the beginner, while more experienced fly fishers can hunt the few larger fish. There are rumors of a few browns in the Downie, though I've yet to catch one.

Lavezzola Creek, near the First Divide. This deep pool might hold a big rainbow.

The Downie River is reached by staying left in Downieville on Main Street for 0.2 miles, then forking left on Gold Bluff Road. If you stay on this road, it dead-ends at a locked barrier. The Downie is broad and shallow here, with little cover, but just upstream is the junction with Lavezzola Creek, above which the fishing improves. You can reach the upper reaches by turning left on Sailor Ravine Road, 200 yards beyond the Gold Bluff Road fork. This very narrow, winding road parallels the Downie upstream for 4.5 miles. The first mile, to Sailor Ravine, is drivable by trucks or even passenger cars, and you could turn or park there. Beyond that, it's a slow, bumpy four-wheel-drive road that will take more than half an hour to negotiate to the end, where there's a parking area for the Downie River Trail, which leads upstream.

LAVEZZOLA CREEK

DeLorme: p. 70, C1–D1
USFS: Tahoe National Forest
USGS: Gold Lake, Mt. Fillmore, Downieville
Altitude: 5200–3100 feet
Water types: Pools, runs, and pocket water.
Trout: Rainbows, 7–12 inches, a few bigger.

Lavezzola Creek is just as pretty as the Downie, but interestingly different. Its deep canyon is initially separated from neighboring Pauley Creek by a narrow, forested ridge interrupted by gaps called "Divides" that carry the dirt road that winds upstream to Lavezzola Ranch and that give us our landmarks. Almost unique among small Sierra streams, it's designated as part of the Wild Trout Program, though this is more symbolic than significant, since the limit remains five fish of any size. This might not matter much, because although the trout population seemed a little depressed in 1997, the heavy flows of the previous winter were probably more to blame than any fishing pressure. The headwaters of Lavezzola Creek are a long way from any road, though a trail does follow it. The middle section can be reached by a short hike, and you can even park at the bridge at the Second Divide and fish right there.

The rainbows that inhabit Lavezzola Creek are silvery fish, with a faint lavender-pink stripe, effective camouflage in their brilliant environment. Its pools may be shaded by overhanging dogwoods, maples, or Indian rhubarb, but they're illuminated by reflected light that bounces off the silvery-gray slate, pale sand, and golden-tan and green cobbles. The water has a slight aquamarine tinge and the gleam of crystal. Occasionally you can see a trout, seemingly suspended in air, but mostly you'd swear there were none present. Then you make a cast, and a trout comes from nowhere, like a conjuring trick. It seems to materialize beneath the fly, as if coalescing from water into a fish.

A miner who spends a lot of time under water in a diver's wet suit told me that he'd seen an 18-inch trout in one pool, and since he used to be a fly fisherman, we can assume it was at least 15. I once hooked and lost a fish about that size myself, though it could have been a brown trout. Whether they've since been removed by anglers or driven out by miners' dredging, I can't say. Fly selection doesn't seem very important, though strangely for such a clear stream, attractor dries like Trudes and Humpies seem to work slightly better than drab, imitative ones like the Adams. In the fall, however, the water gets cruelly cold, and the hatches contract to midges and more midges. Then you can spot fish holding in smooth runs and tailouts, and tiny dries or midge pupae will catch them.

To reach Lavezzola Creek, take Main Street north from Downieville to the new Hospital Bridge across the Downie River. The road bends left, then you take a fork right onto Lavezzola Lane, a good dirt road going uphill. In 1.5 miles, you'll come to the First Divide, from which you can see into both Lavezzola and Pauley Creek canyons simultaneously. There is a chain-link fence and gate on your left, and if you walk around that, an old miners' road will take you upstream for about half a mile before it drops down to the creek. You can't fish upstream very far before some rock climbing becomes necessary, but faint miners' trails go downstream a long way on the south bank, then continue on the north bank. If you stay on the road for 1.3 miles, you'll cross a bridge and can fish either upstream or downstream. The parking area for the Third Divide Trail is 0.7 miles from the bridge, while the trailhead is on Empire Ranch property, a quarter of a mile up the road. The trail crosses Lavezzola Creek on a sturdy footbridge, and you can fish upstream or downstream. If you stay on the county road uphill through the ranch property, you can park by a locked gate in a mile and hike the now private road as it drops back down through a large meadow to the creek. The topo map shows a trail going upstream, though I haven't hiked it yet.

PAULEY CREEK
DeLorme: p. 70, C2–D1
USFS: Tahoe National Forest
USGS: Downieville, Sierra City, Gold Lake
Altitude: 6000–3100 feet
Water types: Pools, runs, and pocket water.
Trout: Rainbows, 7–12 inches, a few bigger.

Pauley Creek is the third of our trio, and it flows into the Downie just below Hospital Bridge. It forms from small streams and springs in broad Gold Valley, then falls quite steeply through a narrow canyon before slowing down a little after Butcher Ranch Creek joins it, substantially increasing its flow. Here it flows southwest through an old-growth redwood and fir forest, then again through a narrow canyon westward to the

*Pauley Creek, near Butcher Ranch Creek. A hikers' paradise,
where you'll find beautifully marked wild rainbows.*

Second Divide, where it turns to the south again and flows roughly parallel to Lavezzola Creek. The lower canyon is rather different to Lavezzola's, being a little drier, its slopes cloaked in oak and manzanita, as well as in fir trees, and its pools deep and steep-sided. Miners work it just as heavily, though.

The rainbows that inhabit the lower canyon are silvery like those of Lavezzola Creek, while up toward Butcher Ranch Creek they have brownish backs and a narrow, deep-red stripe with a tint of gold above and below it, reflecting the change in their surroundings. The lower reaches are often sunlit, and the rocks are a pale gray, while upstream, alders and maples grow close over the westward-flowing stream, keeping it shady for much of the day. Ferns and Indian rhubarb line the banks of long pools and shallow runs among the brown, irregular boulders. These rocks carry an amazing variety of insect life, but as with Lavezzola Creek, the fly pattern you fish seems fairly unimportant. The premium is on predicting where the fish might be and making an accurate cast, the first one always giving you the best chance of success.

The first access is just across Hospital Bridge, where a trail goes to Pauley Falls, just behind the PG&E substation. From there, you can also hike the new First Divide Trail, completed in 1997, which runs high above the creek to join an old miners' road that starts at the First Divide, opposite the chain-link fence. From both trail and road, faint trails lead down to the creek. If you drive Lavezzola Lane for 2.4 miles, you'll come to the Second Divide Trailhead. Park there and hike the trail for just over a mile to a Y junction. If you stay right at the junction, the trail drops downhill a third of a mile to an old miner's cabin, with good water upstream and downstream. Some minor rock climbing may prove necessary through here. If you stay left, the trail gradually drops closer to the stream at various points as it approaches the Third Divide Trail, but that is 4 miles from the trailhead. You could reach that point a little quicker on the Third Divide Trail itself, just over 2 miles from the trailhead, or from Butcher Ranch Creek, the shortest hike, but also the steepest. (See the next listing.) Finally, Gold Valley can be reached by driving the dirt road beyond the Butcher Ranch off-highway vehicle trail 3.4 miles to a designated OHV trail on the left, signposted "Gold Valley 1.5 miles." Since I haven't taken this yet, I'd recommend hiking it, rather than driving it the first time.

BUTCHER RANCH CREEK
DeLorme: p. 70, C/D2
USFS: Tahoe National Forest
USGS: Sierra City
Altitude: 6400–5000 feet
Water types: A little meadow stream, then plunge pools.
Trout: Rainbows, 7–10 inches; brook trout, 7–9 inches.

This little tributary of Pauley Creek is notable for having a population of brook trout, but also for the beauty of its beginnings in a high meadow dotted with wildflowers. The headwaters are choked with brushy alders, but after a large spring triples its flow near the bottom of the meadows, it's a viable fishery. Soon it begins to fall steeply down to Pauley Creek, so steeply that fishing upstream resembles climbing a giant's staircase. You stare into each pool at eye level, while looking downstream can give you vertigo. Rainbows and brookies of some size inhabit these plunge pools, while the headwaters are exclusively the province of little brookies.

It is reached from the east, starting at Bassett's on Highway 49 and taking Gold Lake Road to its junction with Packer Lake Road, where you turn left, then right to Packer Lake. At Packer Lake, fork left on Forest Road 93 (still paved) over Packer Saddle. Then, 0.5 miles from the crest, turn right on a good dirt road signposted to Butcher Ranch Meadow and Gold Valley. In 0.7 miles, a dirt road marked "Butcher Ranch OHV Trail," which is drivable only in a high-clearance four-wheel-drive vehicle, heads steeply down to the left about a mile to the trailhead (stay left at the junction in 0.9 miles). The hiking trail parallels the creek, through the forest and small, brushy meadows fed by springs, for 1.5 miles to its junction with the Pauley Creek Trail. Bear in mind that it falls 1000 feet in this distance, so it's a steep climb out. A second four-wheel-drive road leads into the top meadows 0.5 miles farther downhill, so it can save some extra climbing if you don't have four-wheel drive and have to hike to the trailhead.

GOODYEARS CREEK
DeLorme: p. 69, D7
USFS: Tahoe National Forest
USGS: Downieville, Goodyears Bar
Altitude: 4000–2800 feet
Water types: Little pools and runs.
Trout: Rainbows, 7–10 inches.

Goodyears Creek would be a pleasant place to while away the middle of a summer's day if you were fishing the lower reaches of the North Yuba in the morning and evening. Despite the presence of a large sand-and-gravel works below the bridge, this little creek is very pretty. The prevailing blue-gray slate of the region is interspersed with green serpentine rock, and the banks bear abundant wild roses, lilies, and majestic royal ferns. The trout population is a little sparse in the lower reaches, but they're pretty and plump, sustained by abundant aquatic insects, including plenty of Golden Stones. Shortly after you turn off Highway 49, you will notice a spur road leading to the Goodyears Bar Post Office, a delightful curiosity, since this tiny log cabin is surely the smallest post office you will ever see.

From Highway 49, turn left onto Goodyears Bar Road, just after you cross Goodyears Creek. In 0.6 miles, this road crosses the creek, and you can park there. The road continues upstream for some way, but it enters private property at the end, so I haven't tried to access the headwaters yet. On the other side of Highway 49 are **Rock** and **Woodruff Creeks,** but they're both such trickles by fall that they contain only tiny fish, and they're heavily brushed over, so they're not recommended.

CANYON CREEK
DeLorme: p. 70, C1; p. 69, D6
USFS: Tahoe and Plumas National Forest
USGS: Mt. Fillmore, Goodyears Bar, Strawberry Valley
Altitude: 5200–2300 feet
Water types: Small pools and runs.
Trout: Rainbows 7–10 inches.

I've fished Canyon Creek only once, and I was a little disappointed, though only because I expected it to be a much larger stream than it turned out to be. If you examine maps carefully, you'll note that it drains a large area and flows a very long way to join the North Yuba below Shenanigan Flat. A Forest Service handout about the hiking trail that leads to that junction suggested that it was almost as big as the main river. I haven't hiked to that spot yet, but I have driven to the middle reaches, and it's not even an eighth the flow of the Yuba. That's not to say that it isn't pretty, or that the fishing's terrible, either, and you'll certainly have it to yourself, since it's a long way from anywhere. It rises far to the north, below Beartrap Mountain, close to the headwaters of Lavezzola Creek, and flows southwest for more than 20 miles through a deep canyon. Small rainbows are reasonably common, and 10-inchers hide in occasional deep, shady spots.

It's a pretty stream, particularly striking in fall, when I fished it. Dogwoods and some alders clothe the banks at the bottom of the canyon, beneath a redwood and fir forest. A few mining claims inhabit the middle reaches, and trails do exist that lead down to them, but there is only one road, reached from the Feather River country. From Highway 20, heading east, turn left on Marysville Road, go all the way to La Porte Road, and turn right to Strawberry Valley, then turn right on Forest Road 4, a small paved road signposted to Scales, though the sign is almost illegi-

Lincoln Creek, close to the North Yuba. The tiny plunge pools contain nice trout, if you can beat the brush.

ble. It becomes Forest Road 35, then the pavement ends in about 10.5 miles at a five-way junction. Go straight across on a red dirt road, staying right at a fork in 2.7 miles, and gradually descend into the canyon. You'll pass signs announcing that it's a Plumas National Forest Special Service Road (20N35), and you'll find it drivable in a truck or four-wheel-drive vehicle. It dead-ends at the creek after 4.4 miles, but there is no turn-around at the bottom, so park at a designated campsite on the right in 4.2 miles and walk the last bit, then go through a mining claim to fish upstream. The mouth of Canyon Creek is accessible by a trail from Highway 49. (See the North Fork of the Yuba listing.)

SLATE CREEK
DeLorme: p. 69, B/C7–D6
USFS: Plumas National Forest
USGS: La Porte, Strawberry Valley
Altitude: 5200–2300 feet
Water types: Little pools, pockets, and runs.
Trout: Rainbows, 7–10 inches.

Lower Salmon Lake, Gold Lakes Basin. Best fished in early summer and fall. Bring your float tube.

Slate Creek rises on the other side of Mount Fillmore from Canyon Creek and parallels it the whole way to a junction with the North Yuba. It's more accessible by road, though I've tried it only at the Forest Road 4 crossing. It falls rather more steeply than Canyon Creek at that point and carries more water, so there's better cover for fish. It rushes around big gray-green rocks in a narrow, steep-sided canyon downstream of the bridge. Upstream is private land, though it is not posted. I've fished it so little that it's not fair to report on the fishing quality, but it certainly contains rainbows.

You cross Slate Creek in 3.2 miles on the paved Forest Road 4. (See the Canyon Creek listing.) You could also access it from Scales Road, a fairly rough dirt road that is on the right off La Porte Road, half a mile after Forest Road 4. Many other four-wheel-drive tracks also lead down into its canyon, and it's crossed by County Road 512 from La Porte to Yankee Hill.

LOWER SALMON LAKE
DeLorme: p. 70, C/D2
USFS: Tahoe National Forest
USGS: Gold Lake
Altitude: 6400 feet
Trout: Wild and planted rainbows and brook trout.

The Lakes Basin Recreation Area contains about thirty lakes, more than half in the Feather River drainage, and thus outside the scope of this guide. They all offer good fishing, though several are drive-to lakes that are heavily planted and heavily fished, while others offer a little more solitude and some wild fish. Upper Salmon Lake boasts a resort, with charming cabins reached only by boat. When I drove up to look around, several folks dunked bait next to the boat ramp while families ate their picnics and soaked up the last of the sun. Laughing children splashed each other from inflatable rafts while several small boats weaved among them, trolling for trout. I drove back toward Lower Salmon Lake, inflated my float tube, and walked the half-mile to the lake. I had it all to myself. The trout rose, and I caught two fine rainbows.

Lower Salmon Lake is an ideal size for float tubing. A steep, forested slope falls down to the far (southern) side, while two bare granite peaks dominate the western end. A small inlet stream flows from the gully between them, while another, Salmon Creek, is just to your right. You'll notice that gravel has been added to it to improve the spawning conditions for wild fish. The level, marshy shore indicates the shallows here, while the rest of the lake is mostly of medium depth. The silt bottom, weed beds, and greenish water confirm its fertility. *Callibaetis* mayflies, damselflies, caddisflies, and of course, midges are all present. Fishing will be slow during the day in midsummer, but there will be rising fish in the evening, particularly off the steep bank on the far side. The rainbows are deeply colored, with a bold red stripe, bronzy sheen, and vivid blood-orange fins, and they run 10 to 15 inches. They may be wild, or they may grow on from the fingerlings that are planted here.

To get there, follow Gold Lakes Road from Bassett's for 3.9 miles, then turn left onto a paved road bearing a sign for Salmon Lakes Lodge. In 0.5 miles, you'll see a pullout on the left with a locked green gate and a sign announcing that no motorized boats are allowed on Lower Salmon Lake. A track goes downhill half a mile to the lake.

Upper Sardine Lake, Gold Lakes Basin. This stillwater offers a spectacular view of the Sierra Buttes.

DEER LAKE

DeLorme: p. 70, C/D2
USFS: Tahoe National Forest
USGS: Gold Lake
Altitude: 7100 feet
Trout: Wild and planted brook trout.

Deer Lake is a beautiful high alpine lake with spectacular scenery all around. Climb the slope to the north and look across to the low ridge that dams the south end. There is nothing visible immediately beyond, so the first thing you can see is the Sierra Buttes, like a hanging theater backdrop of distant mountains. Trails, including the Pacific Crest Trail, reach Deer Lake from several directions, and it's a popular hiking destination, so you're unlikely to have it to yourself.

There are some grassy margins that would be shallows early in the season, but most of the shore falls steeply into clear blue depths. On the west side, there is a long island that becomes a promontory when the water drops. Behind it is an enclosed bay, fertile and green with an algal bloom, that would offer good fishing early in the season. *Callibaetis* mayflies and midges certainly are present, together with a few caddisflies. Baby trout can be seen in the margins, but their parents retreat into the depths by midsummer, so you should try to get there by July or postpone a trip until the fall. I believe it was once planted with golden trout, but it has no inlet for spawning, so the ubiquitous brookies have taken over.

The Pacific Crest Trail loops around the east and north shores of the lake, and you could hike that from its crossing of Packer Lakes Road, a quarter of a mile west of Berger Campground. However, this involves a fairly steep, thousand-foot climb, which you can cut in half by entering from Upper Salmon Lake. Follow the directions to Lower Salmon Lake, but continue to the parking area at the end of the road. Walk back 100 yards to the trail, which skirts to the north of Upper Salmon Lake, passes some cabins, and crosses a footbridge over Salmon Creek. In about a quarter of a mile, you will pass tiny Horse Lake, then the trail climbs steeply over a ridge to Deer Lake.

UPPER SARDINE LAKE
DeLorme: p. 70, D2
USFS: Tahoe National Forest
USGS: Sierra City
Altitude: 6000 feet
Trout: Wild and planted rainbows.

Upper Sardine Lake is one of a select number of lakes under consideration for inclusion in the Wild Trout Program by the Department of Fish and Game. It contains trout that are both wild and grown from planted Kamloops rainbow fingerlings, and it's also one of the very few high alpine lakes you can drive straight to and fish. It's also spectacularly lovely. Many of Ansel Adams's famous photos of the Sierra bore no truthful relationship to the actual scenery because he used very long telephoto lenses to make the far-distant mountains seem artificially closer to the foreground subject. He would have hated Upper Sardine Lake, because the Sierra Buttes tower above the lake, so close that you'd have to use one of those disposable panoramic cameras to fit them into even a holiday snapshot.

The trout are silvery, healthy fish from 9 to 14 inches long, with some bigger. Baby trout will be seen in the evenings, sipping the size 38 midges that seem to hatch from such deep, rocky bowls, while larger fish will be hunting emerging caddises closer to shore or feeding on damselfly nymphs and larger midges in the mornings. You could fish from the bank, since it's mostly open, but steep cliffs fall into the lake and make float tubing a more attractive proposition.

A rough, rocky road climbs steeply above Lower Sardine Lake, but though plenty of people seem prepared to walk it and try casual bait dunking at midday, you can have the evening rise to yourself. If you have a high-clearance four-wheel-drive vehicle, you can drive this road. Otherwise, park at the bottom and walk the quarter of a mile. To get there, take Gold Lakes Road at Bassett's, take the first left in 1.2 miles onto Packer Lakes Road, and stay left to Sardine Lakes, continuing to the end of the road at the lodge parking lot.

LODGING IN DOWNIEVILLE

Coyoteville Cabins
(530) 289-3624

Crandall's Riverside Motel
(530) 289-3574

Downieville Motor Inn
(530) 289-3243

Riverside Inn
(530) 289-1000

Robinson's Motel
(530) 289-3573

Saundra Dyer's Resort
Rooms and cottages on the river
(530) 289-3308

Sierra Shangri-La.
Resort with cabins on the river
(530) 289-3455

The Lure
Resort with cabins on the river
(530) 289-3465

For more information, call the Downieville Chamber of Commerce at (530) 289-3507.

LODGING IN SIERRA CITY

Buckhorn Lodge
Motel and family units, restaurant
(530) 862-1170

Busch and Heringlake Inn
Newly restored bed and breakfast
(530) 862-1501

Herrington's Sierra Pines
Rooms and cabins, restaurant
(530) 862-1151

Shannon's Cabins
(530) 862-1287

Sierra Buttes Inn
Hotel, bar, and restaurant
(530) 862-1300

Yuba River Inn
Cabins with kitchens
(530) 862-1122

LODGING IN THE LAKES
BASIN AREA

Bassett's Station
Motel, cafe, and store.
On Highway 49
(530) 862-1297

High Country Inn
Bed and breakfast.
On Highway 49
(530) 862-1530

Packer Lake Lodge
Cabins, bar, and restaurant
(530) 862-1221

Salmon Lake Lodge
Historic cabins reached by boat
(530) 842-3108

Sardine Lake Resort
Restaurant
(530) 862-1196

CAMPSITES

All are National Forest Service
campgrounds unless otherwise stated. Those that charge a fee are
operated by concessionaires and
cost an average of $10 per site. Sites
at those marked with the telephone
symbol ☎ can be reserved by calling 1-800-280-CAMP.

Indian Creek
Highway 49
Private campground,
not suitable for tents
Hot showers, reasonable fee

Carlton Flat
Highway 49
Fee, piped water

Cal-Ida
Off Highway 49
Fee, piped water

Fiddle Creek
Highway 49
Fee, piped water, tents only

Indian Valley
Highway 49
Fee, piped water

Rocky Rest
Highway 49
Fee, piped water

Ramshorn
Highway 49
Fee, piped water

Union Flat
Highway 49
Fee, piped water

Loganville
Highway 49
Fee, piped water

Wild Plum
Wild Plum Road
Fee, piped water

Sierra
Highway 49
Fee, no water

Chapman Creek
Highway 49
Fee, piped water

Yuba Pass ☎
Highway 49
Fee, piped water

Sardine
Sardine Lake
Fee, piped water

Diablo
Packer Lake Road
No fee, no water

Berger
Packer Lake Road
No fee, no water

Packsaddle
Packer Lake Road
Fee, well water, corrals for horses

Salmon Creek
Gold Lake Road
Fee, piped water

Snag Lake
Gold Lake Road
No fee, no water

Undeveloped camping is a rarity in the North Yuba area and specifically prohibited along the river corridor. A very few campsites may be available on the tributaries behind Downieville if not occupied by gold miners. Otherwise, it will be a long, steep climb out of the canyon to the ridge tops before you might find a site.

FLY-FISHING SUPPLIES

Nevada City Anglers
417C Broad Street
Nevada City, CA 95959
(530) 478-9301
Web site: www.goflyfishing.com
The only full-service fly shop nearby.

Bassett's Station
Highway 49 and Gold Lake Road
Bassett's CA 96125
(530) 862-1297
Some flies and tackle.

OTHER SUPPLIES

Groceries and camping supplies are available in Downieville, Sierra City, and at Bassett's Station. Bassett's and Downieville Motors can refill propane tanks, while Downieville Motors also provides hot showers for campers.

Middle Fork of the Yuba River, near Graniteville. A steep hike, but there is trout water at the bottom of the canyon.

THE MIDDLE FORK OF THE YUBA RIVER
DeLorme: p. 80, A4; p. 79, A6
USFS: Tahoe National Forest
USGS: English Mountain, Graniteville, Alleghany, Pike
Altitude: 6800–2400 feet
Water types: Above Jackson Meadows, a little meadow stream. Below Jackson Meadows, tailwater pools and runs, then large pools and riffles.
Trout: Rainbows, 9–16 inches; browns, 10–20 inches; brook trout, 7–9 inches in the headwaters.
Special Regulations: From Jackson Meadows Dam to Milton Reservoir, two trout, maximum size 12 inches, artificial lures with barbless hooks only.

The Middle Fork is the least accessible of the three branches of the Yuba River, and perhaps its most mysterious, too. You may have seen the tailwater that flows into Milton Reservoir, and you may even have caught some nice trout in the early summer, while the hatches are prolific and fish are up from the lake. But if you've glanced over Milton's dam, you'll have observed that the flow is a trickle below. The Middle Fork is badly affected by dams designed to deliver water to the Central Valley, and Milton is merely a storage pond. From there, water goes through the mountain to Bowman Lake by means of a tunnel, and thence into Spaulding Reservoir.

This little-fished river can be divided into three distinct sections. The first has its beginnings in a high valley above Jackson Meadows Reservoir. It's a wide-open little meadow stream there that gets heavily scoured in the spring by snowmelt from the surrounding peaks. The unstable earth banks and low flows in the late summer provide poor cover for fish, but there are little rainbows and brookies to be caught. You'll also get English Meadow all to yourself to admire the many wildflowers, such as violet-blue gentians, peeping through the bright green grass in the spring seeps.

The river below Jackson Meadows Reservoir is a tailwater – a very cold one – that holds a few rainbows and browns all season. Below Milton's dam, the diminished river vanishes into a series of three deep box canyons far from any road access. Streams and springs soon restore the flow, and the deeper pools harbor brown trout of considerable size beneath their vertical cliffs. Getting to them is the challenge. This is also a tailwater, with the cold, fertile water that can support large trout, despite the feeble flows. The browns are active only early in the morning or late in the evening, though, which means you have to backpack into the canyon and spend the night. If you see the river here on a late summer afternoon, crystal-clear water curling slowly around large, pale rocks coated with bright green algae, you'll swear there are no trout. But as soon as the sun dips below the canyon wall, a few small fish appear and start to feed on midges. Then, as the light drops further and mayflies hatch, the big browns appear, fish from 12 inches to as much as 20, ghosting out from beneath the rocks to feed.

Farther down, near Graniteville, the canyon is a little more open, and the flow is a little greater, though ironically, trout still don't seem to be abundant. Down at the first road access, at Tyler Foote Crossing, the trout are more plentiful, all rainbows. They're mostly 9 to 12 inches long, though you'll also find some of the largest rainbows here, particularly early and late in the season. Below the bridge, the river is soon impounded again, at Our House Dam, and more water is removed, so you'll find nothing but a few small rainbows down where Highway 49 crosses the Middle Fork.

Fly-fishing methods have to be tailored to the section you're fishing. The upper meadows might be a good environment for the adventurous beginner fishing with small, general-purpose dry flies, but the other two sections are the province of the experienced hatch matcher. One of the best daytime hatches on the tailwater above Milton is the familiar creamy-orange size 16 mayfly found throughout the Yuba system. Evenings will bring various small, pale-colored duns and a spinner fall. The big pools below Milton also produce mayflies in a bewildering array of sizes and colors, though no one species seems abundant. Smaller caddises in size 18 to 20 are common, and there are always midges hatching in early evening. Golden Stoneflies are present, but only sparsely so. Fall will bring very good hatches of Blue-Winged Olives throughout this section, together with Tricos in the warmer water down toward Tyler Foote Crossing. This is one place where it can be a good idea to carry an imitation of the spent Trico spinner in size 20 to 22. Finally, the box canyons would be good places to fish large streamers at dawn and dusk to try to tempt a real bruiser brown.

The upper meadows can be reached only by a bumpy dirt road not suitable for passenger cars, and then only by some hiking after that. From Jackson Meadows Reservoir, cross the dam and continue 3.3 miles to the first junction. Turn left, signposted to Meadow Lake, past Catfish Lake. In roughly a mile, you will see a spur road to the left, which may be blocked by an earth berm. Hike this road and you will find that a trail goes straight ahead, downhill to the Middle Fork, just above the reservoir. To your right is a waterfall tumbling over a steep cliff. Cross the stream and hike the gentler slope opposite to get above the falls. The meadow you will enter is private land, so use this route only to get there, and stay in the stream channel to fish upstream.

The middle section is reached by turning right onto a dirt road just before Jackson Meadows Dam. It's a bit rough, but probably drivable in a passenger car. You can fish upstream from Milton Reservoir. Continuing down the side of Milton, you'll come to the dam, and you could fish below it if there's water being released. If you stay on Henness Pass Road past the turnoff to Milton Reservoir, a good logging road will take you to Alleghany, high above the river canyon. Trails lead down to good, but strenuous, fishing.

The first is at Big Nose Ridge, 6.3 miles from Milton Dam. A rough four-wheel-drive dirt road heads left, down into the canyon, to a gravel bar at the bottom. Washouts can trash this unmaintained road, so without a jeep, you may find it prudent to park in a large pullout at 0.9 miles and hike from there. In 9.8 miles from Jackson Meadows Dam, there is an indistinct gravel road on the left, just past the junction with Forest Road 98 on the right. Again, it's an unmaintained four-wheel-drive track, which leads to a large pullout area in 0.8 miles. The road continues a short way to an old miner's cabin, then a very steep, unmaintained trail continues down to the top of the first box canyon, at Gates of the Antipodes. It's a very strenuous climb out, so it's emphatically not recommended for the elderly or unfit.

The dirt road becomes the paved Ridge Road, then, after another 7.8 miles, you'll come to a dogleg junction, with Alleghany back to the left. From Alleghany, you can reach the river by dirt road through Plumbago, but I haven't driven this way to the river, so I can't offer full directions. Roughly 7 miles past Alleghany is an unmarked dirt road on the left, County Road 294. Turn left at the end of this dirt road, then immediately right, signposted to Tyler Foote Crossing. A dizzying, but good dirt road picks its way down to the bridge over the Middle Fork.

To reach this area from Highway 49, 1.6 miles after you cross the Middle Fork of the Yuba heading north, turn right onto a paved county road, signposted to Alleghany and Pike. In 12.9 miles, you'll come to a fork where Alleghany is to the right, but keep left to Forest City, then go immediately right. There's no signpost there, but when the pavement ends in another 8 miles, you'll see a signpost to Jackson Meadows, where you keep right. This is Henness Pass Road.

The south-side accesses are reached as follows. Go north on Highway 49, then, 4.3 miles after you cross the South Fork of the Yuba, turn right onto Tyler Foote Crossing Road (paved), signposted to North Columbia. Just after the Columbia Hill Fire Station, turn left onto a dirt road, signposted to Tyler Foote Crossing. Keep straight ahead at the four-way junction, and you'll be on a very old, very narrow road that clings to the side of the canyon, 2.3 miles down to Tyler Foote Crossing. You can fish upstream a long way, and this is the easiest access on the river, but downstream, heavily posted private property begins in a short distance. If you stay on the paved road, it becomes Backbone Road and turns to dirt near Malakoff Diggins State Park, then continues 10 miles to Graniteville. Just before Graniteville is a cemetery on the right, and just before that is a dirt road on the left. Take that 0.2 miles to a fork and stay right, then fork left on a narrow track (not for passenger cars) that leads down a gully beside a tiny stream 0.3 miles to a parking area. A faint, very steep trail goes down the crest of the open ridge below. In a few hundred yards, you will see an obvious miners' trail going left into the woods. Don't take it, since it soon peters out, but continue a hundred yards to another trail on the left, which switchbacks steeply down to the river. Once again, this is not a place for the elderly or unfit. It's a tough climb out.

EAST FORK CREEK
DeLorme: p. 80, A3/2
USFS: Tahoe National Forest
USGS: Graniteville
Altitude: 5400–4000 feet
Water types: Long, slow pools, then runs and pocket water.
Trout: Rainbows, 7–9 inches; browns, 8–10 inches.

This is not one of the best small streams in the Sierra because the flow drops so low by midsummer. Early in the season, though, it might be a good place for the beginner, since it does contain a lot of small, eager trout in a wide-open channel. The open environment is a clear testament to how much water rushes through the broad flood plain in the early spring. Above the bridge where you access it, East Fork Creek runs quite slowly through long pools in the fairly level, well-forested Poorman Valley. Just above the bridge, the outflow stream from Weaver Lake doubles the flow, which does slightly improve the fishing below there. At the end of the valley, the stream quickly gathers pace before falling steeply through plunge pools to the Middle Fork of the Yuba. Where it first starts to run more swiftly, you'll find some nice pools.

There is only one access, where Forest Road 41 crosses the creek. From Graniteville (see The Middle Fork of the Yuba listing above), go west, staying left at three junctions, onto Forest Road 41, which is a well-graded dirt road. You will pass Pyramid Peak and cross East Fork Creek on a bridge. The road continues to Jackson Meadows Reservoir, so if you wish to reach the stream from there, turn right onto Forest Road 41 just past the dam. You also can reach East Fork Creek from the Bowman Lake area. (See the Weaver Lake listing below.)

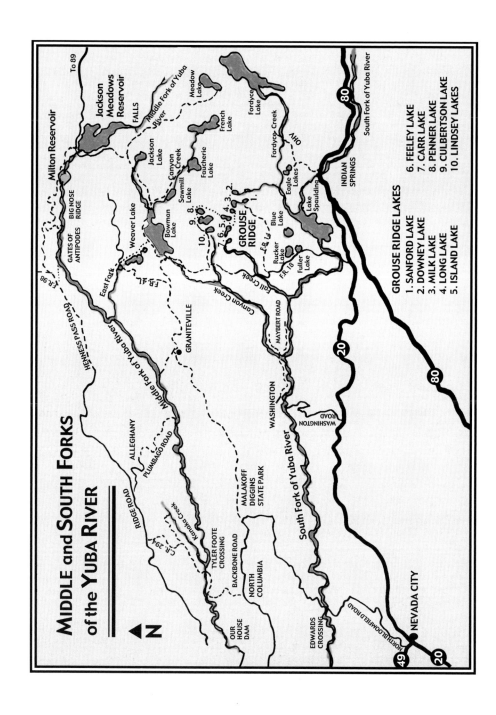

MIDDLE and SOUTH FORKS of the YUBA RIVER

N

To 89

Milton Reservoir

Jackson Meadows Reservoir

FALLS

BIG NOSE RIDGE

GATES OF ANTIPODES

Weaver Lake

East Fork

HENNESS PASS ROAD

Middle Fork of Yuba River

RIDGE ROAD

ALLEGHANY

PLUMBAGO ROAD

Kanaka Creek

C.R. 294

TYLER FOOTE CROSSING

BACKBONE ROAD

NORTH COLUMBIA

OUR HOUSE DAM

MALAKOFF DIGGINS STATE PARK

EDWARDS CROSSING

GRANITEVILLE

F.R. 4

Canyon Creek

WASHINGTON

WASHINGTON ROAD

South Fork of Yuba River

NEVADA CITY

NORTH BLOOMFIELD ROAD

49

20

Middle Fork of Yuba River

Jackson Lake

Canyon Creek

Sawmill Lake

Bowman Lake

French Lake

Faucherie Lake

Fordyce Lake

Fordyce Creek

Eagle Lakes

Lake Spaulding

OHV

GROUSE RIDGE

Blue Lake

Rucker Lake

Fuller Lake

Fall Creek

MAYBERT ROAD

F.R. 18

Meadow Lake

INDIAN SPRINGS

80

20

80

South Fork of Yuba River

GROUSE RIDGE LAKES

1. SANFORD LAKE
2. DOWNEY LAKE
3. MILK LAKE
4. LONG LAKE
5. ISLAND LAKE

6. FEELEY LAKE
7. CARR LAKE
8. PENNER LAKE
9. CULBERTSON LAKE
10. LINDSEY LAKES

KANAKA CREEK
DeLorme: p. 80, A1; p. 79, A7
USFS: Tahoe National Forest
USGS: Pike
Altitude: 4200–2600 feet
Water types: Tiny pools and pocket water.
Trout: Rainbows, 7–10 inches.

This tiny creek offers a pleasant diversion from the Middle Fork of the Yuba in the middle of a hot afternoon. It joins the main river above the bridge at Tyler Foote Crossing, and its narrow canyon heads briefly north, then east. The nearly vertical, mossy rock walls keep the sun out, except at high noon in midsummer—which is not the best time of year to be there, anyway. In the shady, cool stream, small rainbows hide wherever there's any depth to provide cover. It's a lovely challenge for a small-stream enthusiast, since there are fish as big as the average trout one gets in the main river. Take a short 3-weight rod, stealth, a supply of small attractor flies such as the Adams, plenty of drinking water, and did I mention stealth? They're spooky!

You will find the mouth of Kanaka Creek a half mile or so above the bridge at Tyler Foote Crossing. (See the Middle Fork of the Yuba listing for directions.) You can get straight to it by a miners' trail that runs high above the river on the north side, starting at the first bend in the road beyond the bridge. You could also try fishing this tiny creek farther up, behind Alleghany.

OREGON CREEK
DeLorme: p. 79, A7/6
USFS: Tahoe National Forest
USGS: Camptonville
Altitude: 4200–1900 feet
Water types: Little pools and runs.
Trout: Rainbows, 6–8 inches.

I'm listing this little low-elevation stream only in order to suggest you don't bother to fish it, except perhaps in early season. Since it's full of baby rainbows, I assume that it's a spawning stream, possibly even for fish coming up from Englebright Lake. It is pretty, framed by alders and maple and flowing slowly past big sheets of blue-gray slate and thick stands of Indian rhubarb. The insect life is mostly confined to small mayflies and midges, testament to how it warms up in midsummer. However, I've fished it only behind Camptonville, on Pike Road, and there may be cooler water and better fishing farther upstream.

MILTON RESERVOIR
DeLorme: p. 70, D3
USFS: Tahoe National Forest
USGS: Haypress Valley
Altitude: 5700 feet
Trout: Wild browns and rainbows.
Special Regulations: two trout, maximum size 12 inches, artificial lures with barbless hooks only.

Milton Reservoir, also known as Milton Lake, is one of California's designated Wild Trout Lakes. It's an artificial fishery, really, created by cold water fed in from Jackson Meadows Reservoir through the Middle Fork of the Yuba. This is a true tailwater, with flows usually so cold that the surface temperature of Milton can be down in the fifties on an August evening, when any natural lake would be giving off steam as cold air settled over its seventy-degree water. Fly fishing is the only game here, and a float tube is the best way to do it, but you'll need neoprene waders and warm underwear.

In 1992, the dam was leaking a bit, so the whole lake was drained to repair it, and while it was down, the opportunity was taken to improve the bottom habitat. Brush and rock piles were installed as crayfish condos and channels were dredged in the shallow flats. While this was happening, fly fishers worried about the trout, because all the mature fish had been transferred to other lakes nearby. Fingerling browns from two different stocks were reintroduced in 1993, though, and plenty of adult trout must have run upstream into the Middle Fork, then dropped back into the lake, because wild rainbows have turned up, too.

Milton is not a big lake, just twelve acres, so you could kick your float tube around the whole thing in an evening. It might not be a natural lake, but you'd never know it at a casual glance. It's always kept brim full, and the river cuts a channel through broad meadows at the top end, which often are partially flooded, so the decaying grass produces a bumper crop of aquatic insects. You can find fish cruising in the evening or holding station and rising in the slight flow spreading out from the river's mouth. They'll be eating small midges, which can make them frustratingly difficult to catch. The best time to fish can be from midmorning on, which is unusual, but that's when the grayish, speckled-wing *Callibaetis* mayflies start to hatch. Trout will cruise the cool surface layers for much of the day hunting the emerging duns and then the spinners. The rest of the lake is surrounded by rocky, pine-clad banks that fall more steeply into the water, but nowhere is it very deep. These shores are where you're more likely to find some caddis activity in the evening, which may be a better bet for big fish. Nymph fishing is a great method to select, too, particularly with Pheasant Tail or *Callibaetis* Nymphs, if you can bear to ignore all those rising trout. Early in the season, there may be a fall of big flying ants, which led to the development of a giant ant pattern called the Milton Monstrosity.

To get to Milton, take Highway 89 north, then turn left onto the paved Henness Pass Road to its end at Jackson Meadows Reservoir. Just before the Jackson Meadows Dam, on the right, is the dirt road to Milton. It's a bumpy mile, but could be driven carefully in a passenger car. To reach this area from Highway 49, 1.6 miles after you cross the Middle Fork of the Yuba heading north, turn right onto a paved county road, signposted to Alleghany and Pike. In 12.9 miles, you'll come to a fork where Alleghany is to the right, but keep left to Forest City, then go immediately right. There's no signpost there, but when the pavement ends in another 8 miles, you'll see a signpost to Jackson Meadows, where you keep right. This is Henness Pass Road.

WEAVER LAKE
DeLorme: p. 80, A2
USFS: Tahoe National Forest
USGS: Graniteville
Altitude: 5700 feet
Trout: Planted rainbows, brook trout, plus lake trout and some wild browns.

Weaver Lake isn't an outstanding fishery, since most of the trout are planted rainbows. However, some of the mature browns that were transferred from Milton came here, and it's just as fertile, plus bigger and deeper, with the added bonus of a substantial minnow population. When I surveyed Weaver Lake in 1997, something very large was hammering minnows in the channel by the dam, and it doesn't take a genius to figure out what it was, though this self-appointed genius couldn't catch it.

It's also an attractive lake, surrounded by aspens and pine trees, and it's usually quite full. *Callibaetis* mayflies, damselflies, caddisflies, and even some *Baetis* mayflies are all present. There are nice campsites too, even a rest room, so it makes a pleasant base for a fishing expedition. The only drawback is the hideous road in, if you want to come from Interstate 80. Take the Emigrant Gap exit to Highway 20, then turn right onto Bowman Road to Bowman Lake. This is the first paved road you come to, but it's not currently marked except by a brown sign for the Sierra Discovery Trail. The pavement turns to dirt after Clear Creek, then the road becomes worse and worse and . . . you get the picture. Don't come in your Cadillac—this road is four-wheel-drive only. After a bone-shaking ride you come to Bowman, and a quarter of a mile past the dam on the left is another rocky road, signposted to Weaver Lake. You'll pass little McMurray Lake and reach Weaver Lake in a mile. The other options are to come from Jackson Meadows, but the road is just as bad, or to come through Graniteville from Highway 49. (See the directions for East Fork Creek.)

THE SOUTH FORK OF THE YUBA RIVER

DeLorme: p. 81, B5; p. 79, B5
USFS: Tahoe National Forest
USGS: Cisco Grove, Blue Canyon, Washington, North Bloomfield
Altitude: 6500–1300 feet
Water types: Pools, runs and pockets.
Trout: Rainbows, 9–15 inches; browns, 10–15 inches, some bigger.

The South Fork of the Yuba is another enigma. It's like an iceberg, really: you see only a tiny bit of it alongside Interstate 80, where there's little danger of catching any wild trout. The bit you don't see is much more significant, and that's where the decent fishing is. It starts as some tiny, steeply falling little tributaries that join at Soda Springs. You may have seen the big, slow pools downstream when you were driving to Truckee. The river is close to the highway for many miles—indeed, the road crosses and recrosses it a couple of times. This section is often the venue

South Fork of the Yuba River, Maybert Road. This river offers runs and plunge pools for early summer angling.

for happy family groups dunking bait close to the cabins, resorts, and camp-grounds.

The Department of Fish and Game provides plenty of hatchery rainbows here, though a few browns are caught early in the season. If you see it in the fall, you'll understand why it provides poor fishing. A tiny knot of current will push into the long pools, disturbing the placid surface for maybe nine inches or so. Things get a bit better downstream of the small bridge below Indian Springs Campground, where the river falls more steeply and there are some large plunge pools. Then it goes through a few nice runs and riffles before slowing into some deep, sandy-bottomed pools near Spaulding Reservoir. This section produces some fairly large browns, particularly early and late in the season.

Below Spaulding Reservoir, the river looks like a trickle, since most of the water goes down a canal that you cross on Highway 20. However, this is where the South Fork of the Yuba vanishes into its canyon, and the farther you go, the more tributaries add to the flow and the better the fishing gets. Wild rainbows start to show up in quantity through here, and there is access down at Washington. The river is faster, with pocket water and runs in many sections, along with some slower pools in a slightly broader flood plain. The canyon slopes quite steeply, but its sides are fully clothed with pine and fir trees, while large alders and cottonwoods flank the river. There were three thriving towns along Maybert Road during the Gold Rush, and seventeen million dollars in gold was extracted from the canyon over a thirty-year period. Today, there's hardly a sign of any of that, just vine-covered piles of rock turned over by miners in search of their dream beneath.

Downstream of Washington, in the South Yuba Recreation Area, the trout will probably all be rainbows, silvery fish that may be of steelhead ancestry and that will set your reel screaming if you hook one. But the angling starts to become a bit seasonal, since the water warms a little by late summer. Below Edwards Crossing, it gets really marginal, except early and late in the season at Bridgeport for runs of spawning trout from Englebright Lake. Streamers are the pattern to use if you want to fish there. Elsewhere on the river, general dry flies like the Elk Hair Caddis, Humpy, or Adams will work fine. The canyon is a pretty good place for beginners, with plenty of opportunistic fish from 9 to 14 inches, plenty of casting room, and not much fishing pressure. For the hatch matcher, a wide variety of mayflies are present, with a good Blue-Winged Olive hatch at midday in the fall. Caddisflies are abundant too, and Golden Stones in the early summer—a big Yellow or Orange Stimulator is a fine way to sort out a larger rainbow in June. Nymph fishing always works, of course, but you don't have to do it, since it's excellent dry-fly water. The only problem can be low flows from the midsummer onward.

To access the stretch above Spaulding, exit Interstate 80 at the Eagle Lakes turnoff. Continue past Indian Springs Campground to the bridge. You can fish there. If you carry on, the pavement turns to dirt, and you continue under the power line, then fork right over a tiny stream 0.2 miles to a big pullout. Park there, unless you have four-wheel drive. It's 0.5 miles downhill to parking at a rough campsite alongside the river. Big pools and runs are downstream, plunge pools and some riffles upstream.

To get to Washington, take Highway 20 east and turn left onto Washington Road, which winds down to that quaint, historic community. Cross the river and bear right on Maybert Road. This dirt road leads to Keleher Picnic Ground in a mile, then Golden Quartz Picnic Ground in another 2.2 miles. You can park at either. They have rest rooms, but no camping. The dirt road continues some way past Golden Quartz, but it's a track for four-wheel-drive vehicles only. The next access is in the South Yuba Recreation Area. From Nevada City, take Highway 49 north, then the second right onto North Bloomfield Road. Turn right at a stop sign in 0.5 miles, and it's 6 miles to the bridge over the South Fork of the Yuba. Fish there, or continue on the dirt road 1.3 miles to the Bureau of Land Management campground. From there, the South Yuba Trail goes upstream many miles. After a mile, you come to a fork in the trail, and the right branch goes to the river in half a mile.

FORDYCE CREEK
DeLorme: p. 80, B3
USFS: Tahoe National Forest
USGS: Cisco Grove
Altitude: 6400–5000 feet
Water types: Pools, runs, and pocket water.
Trout: Rainbows, 8–14 inches, plus some browns.

Fordyce Creek enjoyed some notoriety for a long time as one of the better creeks in this part of the Sierra. The only thing wrong with that assessment is the use of the term "creek." This "creek" usually carries more water than any one of about six forks of so-called "rivers." It is in fact another tailwater, though it looks and fishes more like a natural freestone stream. It exits Fordyce Lake and flows just 8 miles to Spaulding. A little hiking is involved to get there, but it isn't particularly strenuous fishing, since the elevation doesn't change too steeply.

It's a pretty stream, flowing around small granite domes, with pine trees, flowering shrubs, and ground-covering berry plants beneath. More than half of the river's bed is small cobble that provides a habitat for insect life, but the rest is mostly sandy-bottomed pools, which may be why the trout population has seemed a little sparse whenever I fished it. On the other hand, they may have been flushed out by the many wet winters we've had since 1994. I'd like to see special regulations introduced here, because evidence suggests it sees quite a lot of bait-fishing pressure.

This is not a particularly easy stream to fish. The best pools have conflicting currents where the trout hold, making surface fishing tough, though the fish are keen to come to the surface for food if you can get a good drift. Larger patterns such as Elk Hair Caddises and Humpies seem to bring the best response, but nymph fishing will probably catch more fish.

Some stretches of pocket water can be found, and these stretches may offer the best fishing, but you'll also find long, slow pools where the trout will be sipping small mayfly emergers. There are populations of both caddisflies and mayflies, including the Creamy-Orange Dun found throughout the Yuba system, and some Golden Stoneflies, as well.

The easiest access is by trail from Eagle Lakes. Exit Interstate 80 onto Eagle Lakes Road and continue past the campground. Fork right onto a dirt road, drive to the parking area, and, unless you have four-wheel drive, park there. Otherwise, continue straight on under the power line, then stay right at the first junction. This is a really rough, rocky road that a sport utility vehicle or four-wheel-drive truck can take most of the way to the lakes, while a jeep can get the whole way there. I find it prudent to park in 1.2 miles, just at the end of a level section where the road is deeply cut through the earth, with trees close on both sides. You'll find a couple of pullouts there, just before the road climbs steeply over bare rock. It's about half a mile to Eagle Lakes, staying left at a junction that's signposted. The trail then stays to the left of the first lake and crosses the narrow isthmus between it and the next lake. You'll come to a bridge over the stream. Back on the jeep road, if you stay right, it continues about 2 miles down to the stream.

CANYON CREEK
DeLorme: p. 80, A3–A/B2
USFS: Tahoe National Forest
USGS: English Mountain, Graniteville, Blue Canyon
Altitude: 6600–3100 feet
Water types: Small plunge pools, long pools and runs.
Trout: Rainbows, 8–11 inches; browns, 9–12 inches.

Canyon Creek provides several different fisheries throughout its length. It starts as the outflow of French Lake, flowing in plunge pools and long runs a mile and a half to Faucherie Lake, falling five hundred feet in this distance. This is open, high alpine terrain, with some willow cover along the stream and occasional groves of pines. From Faucherie to Sawmill Lake it flows through long, placid pools between sheets of ledge rock in a pine and fir forest, falling just two hundred and fifty feet in 2 miles. From Sawmill to Bowman Lake, it falls steeply again, then, below Bowman, it goes into the long, deep canyon that gives it its name.

The topmost section offers fun fishing for rainbows and some browns, as does the short piece from Sawmill to Bowman. The middle section, between Faucherie and Sawmill, is challenging water, since many of the long pools are almost still. Browns inhabit every pool through here, and the best fishing will occur during early summer hatches. I have little experience of the canyon section. Down where it joins the South Fork of the Yuba above Washington, it falls very steeply through plunge pools and is heavily posted by miners who work it. National forest land can be reached by hiking the trail on the left just before Golden Quartz Picnic Ground.

The road from Bowman Lake leads to the upper reaches if you stay to the right in Jackson Creek Campground. It goes around a hill and parallels the stream from Sawmill to Faucherie. (Washouts on this road mean that you currently need four-wheel drive to travel it.) To get above Faucherie Lake, cross the stream below the lake, and you'll find a jeep road that goes along the north shore of the lake, almost to the inlet of Canyon Creek. The lower reaches are accessed off Maybert Road. (See the South Fork of the Yuba listing for directions.)

FAUCHERIE LAKE
DeLorme: p. 80, A3
USFS: Tahoe National Forest
USGS: English Mountain
Altitude: 6100 feet
Trout: Planted and wild rainbows and browns.

Faucherie isn't a prolific fishery, but it is one of the loveliest alpine lakes that you can actually drive to and fish. It nestles in a large granite bowl surrounded by high peaks, with waterfalls where the streams flow in. It does see quite a bit of bait-fishing pressure, since it's a popular camping destination, so the Department of Fish and Game plants several thousand fingerling rainbows and browns every year. The size and depth of the lake gives them a chance to grow quite large, and they join a fair population of wild fish born in Canyon Creek. The sides of the lake fall steeply, so a boat or float tube is by far the best way to fly fish it. For directions, see the Canyon Creek listing, above.

FULLER LAKE
DeLorme: p. 80, B2
USFS: Tahoe National Forest
USGS: Blue Canyon
Altitude: 5400 feet
Trout: Wild and planted browns, planted and some wild rainbows.

Fuller Lake is the kind of lake that I normally wouldn't recommend. It's not at a very high elevation, gets heavy bait-fishing pressure, has a private resort on its banks, and is full of planted, catchable-sized rainbows. All these are good reasons for the fly fisher to ignore it. But get there early in the season and paddle your float tube out from the day-use area at the top end, toward the far bank. In fifteen minutes, you'll find yourself in the middle of the lake, carried there by the substantial current from the inflow stream. This stream is really a canal, carrying water from Bowman Lake to Spaulding Reservoir, and its water keeps the lake cool and sustains a population of brown trout from 10 to 15 inches, occasionally bigger. Some are wild, while many are introduced as fingerlings. It's quite pretty, the banks fully clothed with pine and fir trees, with a few willows in the margins. The best fishing is through the early summer and again in the fall. Browns will cruise the bank, hunting for wind-blown terrestrials and emerging caddises, or hold in the current from the inflow stream. This stream brings down all sorts of hatching insects, both mayflies and caddisflies, and the browns queue up to eat them, spread out all the way back into the main body of the lake. Occasional wild rainbows will turn up among them, together with catchable-size planted fish. After the early season hatches, the lake has the usual stillwater insects such as *Callibaetis* mayflies and damselflies.

To get there, take the Emigrant Gap exit off Interstate 80 and take Highway 20 west again, then turn right on the first paved road, which is Bowman Road. The road is not marked, but there is a brown sign for the Sierra Discovery Trail. You'll come to Fuller Lake on your right in 4.0 miles. The first entrance is to the tiny campground and boat ramp by the dam. Continue a few hundred yards, and another dirt road on your right leads down to a day-use area with a rest room and picnic tables, which is the best place to launch a float tube.

THE GROUSE RIDGE LAKES
DeLorme: p. 80, A/B2–3
USFS: Tahoe National Forest
USGS: English Mountain, Graniteville
Altitude: 6400–7000 feet
Trout: Planted and wild rainbows and brook trout.

The Grouse Ridge area has been specifically set aside for backpackers. Some years ago, all the jeep trails were closed to vehicles, and now the only access to the many nice lakes here is by foot or horseback. It's a good place for a first backpacking trip, since this is a relatively level plateau. In fact, if you start from Grouse Ridge Campground, you'll find it's higher than any of your prospective destinations, so the hike in is downhill with a full pack, a considerable benefit if you're new to the game. The views from Grouse Ridge itself are well worth the price of admission. To the west, beyond Island Lake, you see the imposing Fall Creek Mountain, and behind that a series of overlapping ridges receding for 30 miles or more through lighter and lighter shades of blue-gray. To the northwest are the strange, jagged teeth of Bowman Mountain, while to the east, there may be thunderheads over Nevada throwing the orange rock of Old Man Mountain into sharp relief and adding drama to Black Butte.

The only thing that prevents this being a perfect destination is the fact that the lakes get a little warm by midsummer. Trout will still feed in the early morning, though, and just before dark. Most lakes aren't great wild-trout fisheries, since the streams that connect them are seasonal, but many are fertile enough to allow the planted rainbows and brookies to get to respectable size. A float tube might be an advantage, though the banks are often open enough to allow casting. *Callibaetis* mayflies, caddisflies, and damselflies are all present, and small midges are abundant, of course. Watch out for windblown terrestrials, too. They can be important here in the mornings.

You get to the Grouse Ridge area off Bowman Road. (See the Fuller Lake listing above.) Turn right after Trap Creek onto Forest Road 14, signposted to Grouse Ridge. It's 4 miles of good dirt road to the campground. Well-marked trails lead to the lakes.

These are the lakes I've surveyed that are a short hike from Grouse Ridge.

Round Lake
A small, deep lake that requires a float tube.
Milk Lake
Some casting room, but a float tube helps. Fairly shallow.
Long Lake
A small, narrow lake. Some casting room and fairly shallow.
Island Lake
A large, pretty lake with casting room, sizable rainbows.
Downey Lake
Steep rocky banks, but open casting, sizable rainbows.
Sanford Lake
A small, pretty lake with some casting room.

Feeley and the **Lindsey Lakes** you can drive to, and they're reputed to be good fishing, as are **Culbertson** and **Penner Lakes**, a short hike from the Lindsey Lakes. All the lakes receive plants of rainbow or brook trout by air, while some contain wild brookies. **Secret Lake,** to the south of Jackson Meadows, is a short, steep hike, but it's planted with golden trout by air.

Another guidebook recommends fishing the streams here, but they become stagnant pools by midsummer, when they contain catfish, of all things! They might be worth fishing very early in the season. The following lakes should be avoided.

At **Middle Lake,** the dam's gone, and it's a meadow now. **Shotgun Lake** is a marsh full of catfish. **Loney Lake** is very tough to get to, with catfish and few or no trout.

LODGING IN NEVADA CITY

Downie House
Bed and breakfast
1-800-258-2815

Kendall House
Bed and breakfast
(530) 265-0405

Deer Creek Inn
Bed and breakfast
1-800-655-0363

Emma Nevada House
Bed and breakfast
1-800-916-3662

Flume's End
Bed and breakfast
1-800-991-8118

Grand Mere's Inn
Bed and breakfast
(530) 265-4660

M L Marsh House
Bed and breakfast
1-800-874-7458

The Parsonage
Bed and breakfast
(530) 265-9478

Piety Hill Inn
Bed and breakfast
1-800-443-2245

Red Castle
Bed and breakfast
1-800-761-4766

Two Room Inn
Bed and breakfast
1-800-874-7458

US Hotel
Bed and breakfast
1-800-525-4525

Miners' Inn
Restored hotel and cabins
1-800-977-8884

National Hotel
(530) 265-4551

Northern Queen Inn
Motel and restaurant
1-800-226-3090

The Nevada City Chamber of Commerce
(530) 265-2692

Lodging in Grass Valley

Golden Ore House
Bed and breakfast
(530) 272-6872

Murphy's Inn
Bed and breakfast
1-800-895-2488

Best Western Gold Country
Motel
1-800-528-1234

Holiday Lodge
Motel
1-800-742-7125

Holbrooke Hotel
1-800-933-7077

Lodging in Washington

Washington Hotel.
A restored 1857 inn
(530) 265-4364

Campsites: Middle Fork

There are no campgrounds close by the Middle Fork of the Yuba except those at Jackson Meadows Reservoir, which see a lot of use. They're all National Forest Service campgrounds operated by concessionaires and cost an average of $12 per site. Sites can be reserved by calling 1-800-280-CAMP.

East Meadow
Fee, piped water

Findley
Fee, piped water

Fir Top
Fee, piped water

Pass Creek
Fee, piped water

Woodcamp
Fee, piped water

There is an unimproved campground with no water just off Henness Pass Road on Forest Road 98, close to the Gates of the Antipodes. Rough camping is also available at Milton Reservoir and other sites along Henness Pass Road.

Campsites: South Fork

The following campgrounds are found along the South Fork of the Yuba. Unless noted, all are National Forest Service campgrounds operated by concessionaires and cost an average of $12 per site. Sites marked with the telephone icon ☎ can be reserved by calling 1-800-280-CAMP.

South Yuba
Edwards Crossing
BLM,
modest fee, piped water

White Cloud
Highway 20 near Washington
Fee, piped water

River Rest
Washington
Private campground, RVs

Pine Aire
Washington
Private campground, RVs

Indian Springs
Interstate 80, Eagle Lakes exit
Fee, piped water

Big Bend ☎
Interstate 80, Big Bend exit
Fee, piped water

Hampshire Rocks ☎
Interstate 80, Rainbow Road exit
Fee, piped water

The following campgrounds are in the Bowman Road area:

Fuller Lake
On Bowman Road
No fee, no water

Grouse Ridge
Off Bowman Road
No fee, spring water

Bowman Lake
Near far end of the lake
No fee, no water

Jackson Creek
At far end of Bowman
No fee, no water

Canyon Creek
Between Sawmill and Faucherie
No fee, no water

Rough camping is available in the Bowman Lake area, but not near the Yuba's South Fork. Camping is specifically prohibited along Maybert Road at Washington.

FLY-FISHING SUPPLIES

Nevada City Anglers
417C Broad Street
Nevada City, CA 95959
(530) 478-9301
Web site: www.goflyfishing.com
The only full-service fly shop nearby.

OTHER SUPPLIES

For the Middle Fork, groceries and camping supplies are available only in Grass Valley, Nevada City, or North San Juan on Highway 49, so stock up before you head in. If you're fishing the South Fork, some groceries are available in Washington or at gas stations on Interstate 80.

CHAPTER 7: THE AMERICAN RIVER AREA

Study a map of the American River drainage west of Lake Tahoe, and you'll see a network of roads crisscrossing the ridges and valleys between Highway 50 and Interstate 80 like a web of blood vessels. The implication is that access to fishable waters is pretty darn good. And in a way, it is—if you're prepared to drive for hours over washboards and dodge potholes that could do serious harm to the suspension of the average passenger car.

But the sheer abundance of streams here should make even the most chair-bound fly fisher sit up and take notice, then reach for the car keys. There's a lot of water to explore and a very good chance that you'll escape not just from the workaday world, but from other anglers.

Then maybe, just maybe, you'll find a secret place that you can call your own for years to come. I wish you luck.

North Fork of the American River, Sailor Flat. Typically, flows are low here by September.

THE NORTH FORK OF THE AMERICAN RIVER

DeLorme: p. 81, C5; p. 79, D7
USFS: Tahoe National Forest
USGS: Granite Chief, Royal Gorge, Duncan Peak, Westville,
Dutch Flat, Colfax, Greenwood, Auburn
Altitude: 8000–1300 feet
Water types: Pools, riffles, runs, and pocket water.
Trout: Rainbows, 8–15 inches, plus occasional browns.

The North Fork of the American is a designated Wild and Scenic River, preserved by Congress from all development. As you drive Interstate 80 from Sacramento to Truckee, its dramatic canyon is more felt than seen, hinted at only by the occasional glimpse of open space to the south, beyond the pine-covered mountains. Concealed behind these mountains is the quintessential west-slope river, running through one of the deepest canyons in the Sierra. In the spring, abundant snowmelt raises the North Fork to the roaring torrent that carved the canyon. Then, by late summer, it drops to a comparative trickle. But it's not suspicion about the quality of the fishing that causes few fly fishers to visit, it's the serious work involved in getting there. Unless you fish the lower reaches in the spring or fall, down where roads cross it, you're going to have to embark on the hiking adventure of your life, climbing almost three thousand feet into the canyon. And lest we forget, you're going to have to climb out again, albeit with a lighter pack. If there's any history of heart trouble in your family or you wouldn't dream of walking twenty-five flights of stairs to your office if the elevator broke, skip this listing right now. We're talking about climbing those hypothetical twenty-five flights twelve times.

Now that I've thoroughly frightened you, is the trout fishing worth the climb? That depends on your point of view. If you avoid fishing in California because you can fly to Montana, stay in a fancy lodge, and catch big fish without ever walking farther than from the guide's truck to the drift boat, forget it. On the other hand, if you'd like to go and see one of America's most dramatic wild-trout rivers, this may be it. The trout aren't huge, but they're wild, beautiful, abundant, quite easy to catch, and they fight harder than a tailwater rainbow four times their weight. For the young, adventurous beginner or improving fly fisher, this could be a great two-to-four-day trip. The trick is getting there at the right time.

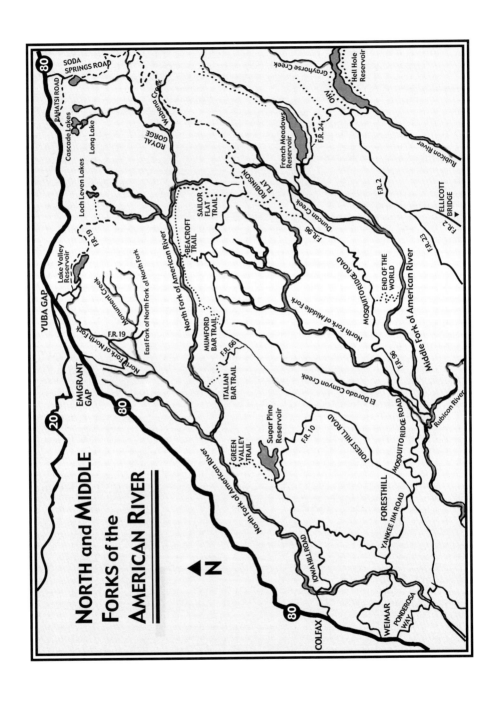

That's from early summer to midsummer, depending on when the runoff ends. There are still plenty of trout in August and September, but when the flow drops, they get pretty spooky.

The North Fork of the American drains the high peaks to the north of the Granite Chief Wilderness. It's just a small stream until it joins its tributaries Cedar, Onion, and Serena Creeks in the sloping valley at The Cedars, where all the land is privately owned. Below Heath Springs, the last trail access for a ways, the river falls over a thousand feet in a mile and a half as it enters the spectacular Royal Gorge. There's a scenic overlook on Soda Springs Road that will give you a taste of the scale and majesty of the North Fork's canyon. Once the river leaves the gorge, a few more tributaries increase the flow, and there are three trails into the canyon at Sailor Flat, then Beacroft, then Mumford Bar. The canyon is a little more open now, and grassy or wooded flats spread above the river's flood plain. Camping spots can be found near the three trails, and they're linked with each other by the 8-mile American River Trail. The abandoned cabins of gold miners can be glimpsed through the trees, revealing who built these trails in the first place. Two more trails give access farther downstream, and I intend to check out the Green Valley Trail, because it reaches the river a mile below the North Fork of the North Fork, a tailwater tributary that I'm guessing cools the river down a bit.

By the time the river reaches the first road access to this canyon, at Iowa Hill Road, it gets a little too warm as flows drop in the middle to late spring. Bill Kiene, of Kiene's Fly Shop, tells me that there is trout fishing in the lower reaches in the spring, before the snow melts, if that holds off until after the season opens, and again in the fall, when the temperatures start to drop. But the North Fork isn't as attractive there. The bottom of the canyon is not much more than a thousand feet above sea level, and it's pointing broadly south, so the sun beats on the river and its canyon all day long. The fir trees that provided shady camping spots upstream are scarce, and gnarled live oaks pay tribute to how hot and dry it gets. The lower river is better known as a smallmouth bass fishery. I'm told that the smallmouth fishing is particularly good below Lake Clementine. (The dam there is a top-water release dam, so it doesn't have a cooling effect on the river's flow that might improve the trout fishing.)

The trout are mostly rainbows, silvery fish that resemble steelhead in both appearance and fighting ability. There are browns, too, though I've yet to catch one. I suspect they lurk in the few really deep holes, driven there as the flow drops. Though there are hatches of mayflies and caddises, general dry-fly patterns such as the Adams, Humpy, and Elk Hair Caddis will work fine in the upper canyon. I wouldn't go there without Golden Stonefly patterns, however, both nymphs and dries, since they can be the best way to pick up a larger fish.

The first road access to the river is from Soda Springs Road, a very long dirt road not recommended for regular passenger cars, that links Interstate 80 with Foresthill Road. Exit I-80 to Norden, then turn first right on Soda Springs Road. Where it crosses the North Fork, all the land is private, but you'll come to Palisade Creek Trailhead, just past the overlook. The other end of this trail is at Cascade Lakes. (See the Long Lake listing below.) The main trails into the canyon, though, are best reached from Foresthill Road, which can be reached by exiting Interstate 80 just northeast of Auburn. Continue on through the town of Foresthill. The first is the Green Valley Trail. Turn left 7 miles from Foresthill onto Forest Road 10 to Sugar Pine Reservoir. Follow this paved road for about 5 miles, go over the dam, then turn left on Elliot Ranch Road. The trailhead is in 3 miles. The Italian Bar Trail is left off Foresthill Road after 12 miles. Take the dirt Humbug Ridge Road (Forest Road 66) for 3 miles. The next two trailheads, Mumford Bar and Beacroft, are immediately off Foresthill Road at 13 and 17 miles. The last trail is at Sailor Flat. Turn left off Foresthill Road and 1.2 miles of high-clearance dirt road leads to a parking area where several tracks divide. The steep, jeep-only road in the middle leads another mile to the trailhead. These trails are described in detail on the Tahoe National Forest Foresthill Trails leaflet, which you can pick up at the Foresthill Ranger Station or order by mail from the Foresthill Ranger District, 22830 Foresthill Road, Foresthill, CA 95631. The trails are correctly described as "Most Difficult" in the leaflet. They all take 80 to 120 minutes on the way in, but more than twice as long on the way out, even if you're very fit. The climb varies from 2400 feet to over 3000. The roads that reach the lower parts of the river are obvious off Interstate 80, and I haven't fished here enough to recommend any one over another. Foresthill Road crosses the river below Lake Clementine, if you want to try for smallmouths.

THE NORTH FORK OF THE NORTH FORK OF THE AMERICAN RIVER

DeLorme: p. 80, B3–C1
USFS: Tahoe National Forest
USGS: Cisco Grove, Blue Canyon
Altitude: 5800–2100 feet
Water types: Small pools, runs, and pocket water.
Trout: Browns, 8–12 inches; rainbows, 6–10 inches.

This is almost the only tributary to the North Fork that's accessible to anglers without some serious hiking, even rock climbing. It's actually a tailwater, and both its strong population of brown trout and the abundance of insect life reflect that fact. It rises in a wooded valley above Lake Valley Reservoir, but it's below the lake that the viable fishing starts, where it pushes strongly through rocky runs and long, placid pools in pretty country. Fishing can be a little challenging there, because the stable flow lets bush alders and willows grow densely along the banks, and they can obstruct your casting. Several miles farther down, the stream is easily accessed where it crosses under a dirt road and runs alongside North Fork Campground. The pools right by the campground are a little too placid and open, and they get planted trout and bait-fishing pressure, but if you walk down into the canyon, the stream falls steeply through rocky plunge pools and the fishing's better.

Near the reservoir, the trout will be nearly all browns, and you may have to go to the trouble of matching hatches and lengthening your tippet. Down by the campground, you'll find an equal number of rainbows and browns, and general fly patterns will usually work just fine. The upper reaches are accessed by turning off Interstate 80 at the Yuba Gap exit, then turning south on Lake Valley Road. Stay right at the fork in 0.3 miles, then turn right on the gated dirt road marked as a dead end just before Forest Road 19. It crosses the stream in a few hundred yards. To reach North Fork Campground, take the Emigrant Gap exit off I-80 and turn immediately right at the T junction onto Emigrant Gap Road, which becomes the paved Forest Road 19. Continue to the campground and park, then I recommend a short hike upstream or downstream to fish.

THE EAST FORK OF THE NORTH FORK OF THE NORTH FORK OF THE AMERICAN RIVER

DeLorme: p. 80, B/C3–B/C2
USFS: Tahoe National Forest
USGS: Duncan Peak, Westville
Altitude: 6500–3600 feet
Water types: Tiny pools, runs, and pocket water.
Trout: Rainbows, 6–9 inches.

Surely this has to be the longest name attached to any stream in California. The East Fork Etc. runs swiftly among golden-colored rocks with an occasional gray boulder for variety, while much of the small cobble in the pools is orange. The banks are heavily clothed with maples, dogwoods, and drifts of white-flowered azaleas. Come here in the second or third week of June and the scent of these lovely flowers will knock your socks off. The size of the trout is hardly spectacular, but they are every bit as lovely as the stream, bright and heavily marked, with vivid white edges on their lower fins. There are plenty of stonefly nymphs under the rocks, just as there are in the North Fork, but a general dry fly will be all that you'll need. To get there, continue beyond North Fork Campground (see above) on Forest Road 19, and you'll cross this little stream at milepost 7 1/2

LONG LAKE

DeLorme: p. 81, B4
USFS: Tahoe National Forest
USGS: Soda Springs
Altitude: 6200 feet
Trout: Planted rainbows.

Long Lake sits in a hanging valley just to the east of dramatic Devil's Peak. As you look down the narrow lake, pinched between low rock cliffs, you have a sense of many cubic miles of air beyond, hanging high above the North Fork of the American, while far off in the distance sit the massed peaks of the Granite Chief Wilderness. As a combined family picnic and casual fishing spot, it's unrivaled, which may be why the Department of Fish and Game goes to the trouble of planting it with fingerling rainbows. The fishing, though, is nowhere near as spectacular as the scenery, since it's too deep and rocky for much in the way of insect life, barring midges, of course.

To get there, turn off Interstate 80 to Norden, take the first right onto Soda Springs Road, then go right onto Pahatsi Road, signposted to Cascade Lakes. The road turns to dirt, then stay right past Palisade and Kidd Lakes toward Cascade Lakes and park on a bluff above the lakes. The Palisade Creek Trail crosses a bridge between them. In a quarter of a mile, stay left where the North Fork is to the right. It's 200 yards to the lake.

THE LOCH LEVEN LAKES
DeLorme: p. 80, B3/4
USFS: Tahoe National Forest
USGS: Cisco Grove
Altitude: 6800 feet
Trout: Planted rainbows and brook trout.

These small, very pretty lakes are said to have provided good brown trout fishing in the past, but I'm at a loss to understand how, since they lack year-round inflow streams. Today they depend on the Department of Fish and Game airplane for baby rainbows and brook trout. They're surrounded by white granite rock with dark speckles, sparsely covered with pine and some juniper. Two different kinds of heather and the fluffy pink flowers of spirea provide quite a display in the late summer. Promontories offer casting room on all of them, but the fishing is a bit spotty. Lower Loch Leven is narrow and mostly deep, Middle Loch Leven is the largest, with several islands, while High Loch Leven is mostly shallow, with one deep area and two islands.

Some volunteer trail mappers I met told me that the Loch Leven Trail was one of the most heavily used in the Sierra. It climbs steeply from Big Bend Campground on Interstate 80, so I took the easy way in, the Salmon Lake Trail, which involves only a hundred feet or so of elevation change. Turn off I-80 at the Yuba Gap exit and head south on Lake Valley Road. Stay right at the fork in 0.3 miles, then turn left onto Forest Road 19, which is graveled here. Pass Lake Valley Reservoir and turn left at the first junction, signposted to Huysink Lake, on a dirt road that is not really recommended for passenger cars. In 0.3 miles, you pass tiny

Upper Loch Leven Lake. An attractive stillwater with spotty fishing. Easily accessed via the Salmon Lake trail.

Huysink Lake, then, in a similar distance, you'll see an indistinct sign for Salmon Lake Trail on your left. Hike the trail over a ridge, cross the outflow of a marshy lake, and stay left at the trail junction in less than a mile, signposted to Loch Leven Lakes. Lower Loch Leven is three-quarters of a mile, the other lakes are each a quarter of a mile farther.

THE MIDDLE FORK OF THE AMERICAN RIVER
DeLorme: p. 81, C5; p. 87, A6
USFS: Tahoe National Forest
USGS: Royal Gorge, Bunker Hill, Greek Store, Michigan Bluff
Altitude: 8200–1300 feet
Water types: Pools, runs, and pocket water.
Trout: Rainbows, 8–15 inches, and some browns.

The Middle Fork of the American differs from the North Fork in only two ways: its canyon isn't quite as deep, and dams control most of its flow. It's also not quite the size of the North Fork, at least until the Rubicon joins it in the lower reaches. Otherwise, it's much like any of the other canyon streams in the area in that it fishes best for a couple of months after the snowmelt ends. However, it is a little more fertile than most west-slope streams. Above French Meadows Reservoir, it runs rather too slowly through a broad flood plain over small cobbles, with little in the way of good holding water. There may be better fishing than I've found, but I wouldn't recommend the stream here, except in the early summer. French Meadows Reservoir is undeniably attractive, though, if you want to go for a family camping trip. However, once the river exits the impoundment, the fishing improves substantially.

The trout in the Middle Fork of the American are mainly rainbows, though there are a few more browns than you'll find in the North Fork. Most of the trout are less than 12 inches, but there are a few of 13 and 14 inches to make it interesting. Browns are slightly more common as you get up near the dam at French Meadows. The insect population is pretty varied, with plenty of small mayflies and caddisflies and lots of Golden Stones. Just as on the North Fork, attractor dry flies will work fine, but fussier patterns are a good idea for the larger pools, and you should always carry Golden Stone dries and nymphs from early summer to midsummer.

To get to the Middle Fork, turn right in the town of Foresthill onto Mosquito Ridge Road (Forest Road 96), signposted to French Meadows Reservoir. There are three road accesses to the Middle Fork from here. In 32.3 miles, at French Meadows Dam, a short dirt road heads downstream. Then, at Middle Fork Powerhouse, 19.3 miles from Foresthill, a paved road on the right winds down to the powerhouse at the bottom of the canyon. Finally, you can fish upstream from Ralston Picnic Area. Turn right off Mosquito Ridge Road at 10.2 miles onto Forest Road 23, signposted to Oxbow Reservoir. It's 1.3 miles downhill to the picnic area. There's also one trail that leads into the canyon, 2.3 miles after the bridge over the North Fork of the Middle Fork on Mosquito Ridge Road. The Mosquito Ridge Trail winds down steeply, 700 feet in a mile and a quarter.

Below Oxbow Reservoir, the Middle Fork looks interesting, and there are rumors of some large rainbows in this dramatic stretch of boiling white water. But there are very few accesses, and they're all on private land. If you try to fish down from Oxbow Reservoir, you come to private land at Horseshoe Bend in about half a mile, and the owner has established that he actually owns the riverbed, so you can't continue downstream. Gary Eblen of The American Fly Fishing Company has fished this stretch, though, by floating it with one the many rafting companies that operate there. He said it was exciting rafting, but he didn't hook any monsters.

DUNCAN CREEK

DeLorme: p. 80, C4–D3
USFS: Tahoe National Forest
USGS: Royal Gorge, Greek Store
Altitude: 8200–1300 feet
Water types: Little pools and runs.
Trout: Rainbows, 6–10 inches, a few browns.

Duncan Creek is a charming little creek, hidden a long way from anywhere that fly fishers usually venture. It's a typical small stream for the area, taking up a lot of space on the map as its long canyon descends slowly toward the Middle Fork of the American. On the ground, it's rather smaller than you might expect, and the flow gets a bit low by late summer. The rocks are gray-green and orange, with plenty of ferns and Indian rhubarb overhanging the pools. The Department of Fish and Game has had reports of brown trout in the headwaters, but fat, sassy rainbows are the more usual inhabitants, and they get to a respectable size. Trout food is abundant, particularly small tan *Glossosoma* caddisflies. To get there, turn right off Interstate 80 to the town of Foresthill. Turn right just before the town center onto the paved Forest Road 96 to French Meadows Reservoir. You'll cross the creek in 29.6 miles. Half a mile before the bridge is a turning on the left that leads to a small hydro dam upstream. You could also reach the headwaters by taking the States Trail from Robinson Flat Campground on Foresthill Road.

THE NORTH FORK OF THE MIDDLE FORK OF THE AMERICAN RIVER

DeLorme: p. 80, C/D3–D2
USFS: Tahoe National Forest
USGS: Duncan Peak, Greek Store, Michigan Bluff, Foresthill, Georgetown, Greenwood
Altitude: 6000–1300 feet
Water types: Pools, runs, and pocket water.
Trout: Rainbows, 6–12 inches.

This is a medium-sized stream that runs almost unnoticed at the bottom of a very deep, steep-sided canyon. If it wasn't for the fact that Forest Road 96 crosses it, no one but gold miners would ever visit. But miners can go to a lot of trouble to get there. I asked how one group got their equipment a few miles upstream and was told "Helicopter"! The extreme depth of the canyon gives a clue as to why this is a better fishery than might be expected at this low elevation. It can be almost cool down on the stream, while the top of the canyon fries in near-hundred-degree weather. Waders would be a mistake, though. Except for early in the season, shorts and wading boots will be all that you'll need. Large mayfly nymphs and Golden Stones are quite abundant, but most of the trout are still 6 to 8 inches long. Perhaps a hike farther up-canyon would bring the reward of more trout like the single 15-incher I caught here.

Coming from Foresthill on Forest Road 96, you'll cross over the North Fork of the Middle Fork in 9.8 miles. A gated road on the west side of the bridge goes down to the river below. On the east side of the bridge is a trail that leads upstream, high above the river, but it comes down to the river in a mile or so, close to the junction with Eldorado Canyon. Please respect the miners' encampments if you need to pass through. Remember that it was miners with hand tools who built this fine trail.

THE RUBICON RIVER
DeLorme: p. 89, A6; p. 88, A2
USFS: Tahoe National Forest / Eldorado National Forest
USGS: Rockbound Valley, Homewood, Wentworth Springs,
Bunker Hill,
Robbs Peak, Devil Peak, Tunnel Hill
Altitude: 8200–1300 feet
Water types: Pools, runs, and pocket water,
Trout: Rainbows, 7–12 inches, a few browns, and in the wilderness
area, brook trout and golden trout.

The rocky Rubicon rises in the very center of the Desolation Wilderness, in the dramatic expanse of Rockbound Valley. Once, this river was a steelhead spawning stream, and migratory fish penetrated high into the heart of the Sierra. The Rubicon runs into the Middle Fork of the American River, and the dams on the American put a stop to the migratory runs. Then Rubicon Reservoir, on the upper reaches of the stream in the Desolation Wilderness, flooded Onion Flat in the early 1960s and reduced this once-fine wild-trout stream to a mere 10 miles of flow above the new reservoir. Hell Hole Reservoir also controls its flow farther down, and below its huge dam, the river flows through a long, deep canyon with few accesses. The extreme depth of Hell Hole means there's little enrichment of this stream below it, compared with many tailwaters. The Rubicon below Hell Hole is a fast-action fishery, a 12-inch trout being a trophy. That makes the middle reaches an ideal place for the beginner, with plenty of eager, small trout prepared to take a dry fly.

Golden trout swim in the topmost reaches, far from any trailhead, where only overnight visitors will fish. Below Rubicon Reservoir, still in the Desolation Wilderness, but approaching a viable day hike, the other species of trout can be found. For trail accesses, see the Desolation Wilderness chapter. You can also reach the stream by a hot, strenuous hike along the north shore of Hell Hole Reservoir. Take the paved Forest Road 2 to Hell Hole, then turn left just past the Forest Service Guard Station, onto Forest Road 24 to French Meadows. Turn immediately right onto the Hell Hole Jeep Trail and park (unless you have a jeep). It's 6 miles to the far end of the reservoir. The jeep road ends at Grayhorse Creek, and the trail beyond is faint, so you may find it best to follow the shoreline the last mile to Five Lakes Creek. The Rubicon is the other side of a steep ridge with only one route through, but high cliffs and a deep pool make it impossible to get up from the lake. The better route may be the Hell Hole Trail on the south side. Park above the dam and cross it to the trail. This is a small stream by late summer, but there are rainbows wherever there's cover.

Below Hell Hole, the only easy access to the canyon is at Ellicott Bridge. Take Highway 193 to Georgetown, either north from Highway 50 or south from Interstate 80. Turn east onto Main Street, which becomes Wentworth Springs Road, then paved Forest Road 1, to Stumpy Meadows Lake. After Stumpy Meadows, turn left in about 5 miles onto paved Forest Road 2, which winds down to Ellicott Bridge. From the parking area on the far, northeast side, a trail follows the stream all the way to Hell Hole Reservoir, 10 miles away. To access the lower reaches, take the Nevada Point Trail. From Georgetown, head east on Wentworth Springs Road, then turn left onto Volcanoville Road, Forest Road 15. In about a mile and a half, turn right onto Rubicon Road. In about 2 miles, a short spur road on the right leads to the trailhead. The trail leads steeply down to the river. You'll find these trails listed on the *Hiking Trails of the Sierra* leaflet obtainable from the Eldorado National Forest.

BARKER CREEK
DeLorme: p. 81, D5/6
USFS: Tahoe National Forest
USGS: Homewood, Wentworth Springs
Altitude: 7500–4800 feet
Water types: A meadow stream, then tiny pools and runs.
Trout: Brook trout, 6–9 inches, and some rainbows.

This is a pretty, but tiny meadow stream in its upper reaches, providing a rare brook-trout-only fishery. The brookies are spooky, and though the stream is too tiny for them to get big, it's a challenge to try to sneak up on trout that you can easily see in the water. They'll take any small dry fly if you can avoid scaring them, and with a decent flow year-round, it's also fishable right through to the fall. It's reached by a long, but very scenic drive from Lake Tahoe. Turn off Highway 89 north of Homewood onto Forest Road 3 to Blackwood Canyon. Take this road up and over Barker Pass until the pavement ends. In 1.7 miles, turn left onto the unsigned Forest Road 3-4. (The views of Rockbound Valley from this road are well worth the drive.) It's 2.2 miles to a bridge over Barker Creek, and the meadow is upstream.

Five Lakes Creek, Granite Chief Wilderness. Reaching this stream requires a hike along the north shore of the well-named Hell Hole Reservoir.

FIVE LAKES CREEK
DeLorme: p. 81, C5–D5
USFS: Tahoe National Forest
USGS: Granite Chief, Wentworth Springs
Altitude: 7500–4600 feet
Water types: Small pools, runs, and pocket water.
Trout: Rainbows, 7–12 inches, plus brook trout in the headwaters.

Five Lakes Creek is the jewel of the Granite Chief Wilderness. The lakes that feed it and give it its name are close to the Alpine Meadows ski area, and they get so much pressure from backpackers that the Forest Service has recently closed them to camping. The creek, on the other hand, runs 12 miles through the wilderness area to Hell Hole Reservoir, passing nowhere near a road of any kind. If you're not prepared to backpack for good small-stream fishing, skip this listing. If you are, this creek is a beauty. It falls fairly steeply through both high, rocky country and dense pine forest, eventually falling over a lovely waterfall just half a mile above Hell Hole. Below the falls, it runs through a boulder field, then a short, narrow little canyon.

The stream is quite fertile, with a good variety of insect life, particularly small caddisflies and Golden Stoneflies. The trout are rainbows throughout most of its length, plump fish, too. Below the falls, you may catch a larger trout that's run up from the reservoir, even late in the season, when the flow is still quite good. You can access the lower reaches by a tough 6-mile hike along the Hell Hole Jeep Trail. (See the Rubicon River listing above.) The middle reaches are definitely only for the overnight visitor, since you'll do a minimum of 1800 feet of climbing. Grayhorse Valley Trailhead leads to the Shanks Cove Trail and the Five Lakes Trail. From Forest Road 24 (see the Rubicon River listing), turn right at the end of the pavement onto Forest Road 48-14 (a track for high-clearance vehicles only), and follow it for 5.5 miles to the trailhead. The Powderhorn Trail leads to Five Lakes Creek from the Lake Tahoe side. The trailhead can be found 1.7 miles from the end of the pavement on Barker Pass Road. (See the Barker Creek listing.) A leaflet on the Granite Chief Wilderness can be obtained from the Forest Service by writing or calling the Foresthill Ranger District or the Truckee Ranger Station. (See the information collected under "Maps" in "How to Get There, Stay There, and Stay Safe") You'll need the topo maps, too.

THE SOUTH FORK OF THE RUBICON RIVER
DeLorme: p. 89, A5; p. 88, A4
USFS: Eldorado National Forest
USGS: Loon Lake, Robbs Peak
Altitude: 6800–4000 feet
Water types: Pools and runs.
Trout: Rainbows, 6–9 inches; browns, 8–12 inches.

The South Fork is a pretty stream in a shallow, wooded valley. It's bordered by Indian rhubarb and alders and flows over sheets of pale granite, carving them into Henry Moore sculptures. It drops to a trickle by late summer, at least above Gerle Creek, which more than doubles the South Fork's flow. Small rainbows are quite plentiful, with sizable browns in the bigger pools. From Highway 50, take Ice House Road (Forest Road 3) and turn left after 23 miles to South Fork Campground. In 2.2 miles, there is a bridge over the South Fork of the Rubicon. Just before it, a spur road on the left leads downstream. You can access the lower reaches, where the trout are all browns, by hiking up the main stem of the Rubicon from Ellicott Bridge.

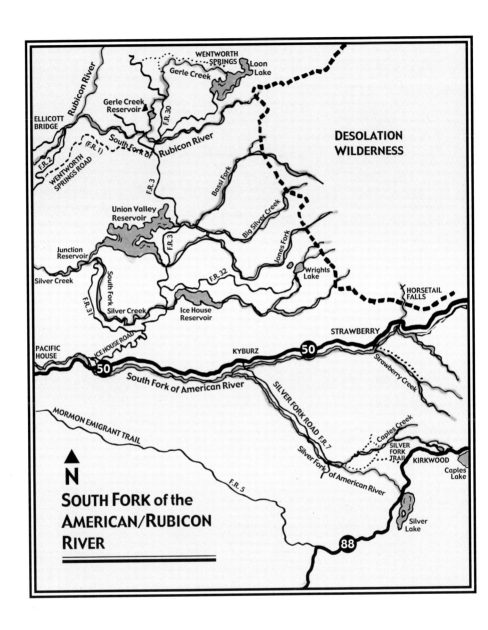

GERLE CREEK
DeLorme: p. 89, A5; p. 81, D5
USFS: Eldorado National Forest
USGS: Wentworth Springs, Bunker Hill, Robbs Peak
Altitude: 6800–5200 feet
Water types: Runs with log structure, then pools and pocket water.
Trout: Browns, 7–11 inches, plus some rainbows and brook trout.

This stream flows strongly all year long because its flow is controlled. You could say there was nothing wrong with that, if it provided good fishing, but that's only intermittently true of Gerle Creek. Where you first see it, by Airport Flat Campground, it flows through long, placid pools created by little man-made dams, apparently designed to give planted rainbows somewhere to mill around aimlessly. Strike out upstream, though, and you'll find some nice pocket water with reasonable numbers of wild browns. The so-called "meadows" in the upper reaches are actually fully grown over with forest, but there is a meadow-type stream with some sizable trout hidden in the jungle. The trouble is, most of the land is private. From Highway 50, take Ice House Road (Forest Road 3) past the South Fork of the Rubicon, then go left on Forest Road 30, where Loon Lake is to the right. You'll cross Gerle Creek just before Airport Flat.

LONG CANYON CREEK
DeLorme: p. 81, D4; p. 88, A2
USFS: Eldorado National Forest
USGS: Bunker Hill, Greek Store, Devil Peak, Tunnel Hill
Altitude: 8200–1300 feet
Water types: Little pools and runs.
Trout: Rainbows, 6–10 inches.

This pretty little stream is very similar to Duncan Creek (see above). The well-named canyon makes you expect a lot more water than the trickle you'll find in the late summer, but it's still full of little trout. Just go early in the season, particularly if you're a beginner. It runs in a V-shaped canyon that's quite easy to get up and down. Aquatic insects are plentiful, but a general dry fly will be quite sufficient. Paved National Forest Service roads cross it at two locations, Forest Road 2, many miles from the Rubicon at

Ellicott Bridge, and the road at Ramsey Crossing that joins Forest Road 2 to Forest Road 23 from Foresthill.

MILLER LAKE
DeLorme: p. 81, D6
USFS: Tahoe National Forest
USGS: Homewood
Altitude: 7100 feet
Trout: Wild and planted brook trout, plus a few rainbows.

Miller Lake is a typical Desolation Wilderness lake, with abundant brook trout. The only difference is, it's not actually in the wilderness area, and you can drive to it with a four-wheel-drive vehicle. It sits in a level valley surrounded by pine trees in a saddle between the Rubicon and Lake Tahoe. It's a popular spot for folks riding the Rubicon Jeep Trail, one of the toughest in California. The lake is an ideal depth, varying from sunlit shallows to twenty feet at its deepest. It's silty and fertile, which produces a varied insect population and plump, pretty brookies. There are some shiner minnows in there, too, so a small streamer will catch the brookies, as well. Fishing gets quite slow in midsummer, though, since the surface warms up and the trout stay deep.

There is shore fishing, particularly from a small meadow on the far side, but a float tube is a better idea. The very few wild rainbows must have come up from the Rubicon in a big snowmelt. If you catch one, please return it, though a brookie could go in the pan without harming the fishery.

The obvious route here is the McKinney / Rubicon Springs Jeep Trail, but this way in is very tough for anything but a jeep. It's 2 seriously bumpy four-wheel-drive miles from the off-highway vehicle staging area at the end of the paved McKinney–Rubicon Springs Road from Highway 89, north of Tahoma. Deep downcutting of this trail near Miller Lake can make it tough for even a four-wheel drive to traverse. The alternative, much longer, but less bumpy route is over Barker Pass. (See the Barker Creek listing.). If you continue on Forest Road 3-4 from the creek, you'll come to Bear Lake in 2.2 miles. Then you need to stay

right in half a mile, right again in another mile, and then stay left immediately. You'll drop down to join the Rubicon Jeep Trail, then turn left for
a mile, past a shallow lily pond, to Miller Lake. Nearby **Bear Lake** is similar, with plenty of sizeable brookies, too. **Richardson Lake** is also report-
ed to provide good fishing for brookies.

GERLE CREEK RESERVOIR
DeLorme: p. 89, A4/5
USFS: Eldorado National Forest
USGS: Robbs Peak
Altitude: 5200 feet
Trout: Wild browns, plus a few rainbows.

This man-made lake is a storage facility in a water-supply system that
takes water stored in Loon Lake and delivers it through Gerle Creek.
Despite that, it's just as pretty as the similar, but better-known Milton
Reservoir in the Yuba drainage, and the fishing's almost as good, too. The
old-fashioned tower on the dam, the rocky islands, and the pine forests
that slope down to every shore make it look like a miniature Scottish loch,
so it's an appropriate place to find wild brown trout. The fishery is set aside
for this self-sustaining population, and despite a busy campground and
the lack of special regulations to protect them, they do just fine.

The lake is of ideal depth. Caddises, Callibaetis mayflies, dam-
selflies, and midges feed the trout, but the pine woods make wind-
blown terrestrials an important part of their diet, too. The browns are pret-
ty, dark-colored, and run 12 to 16 inches, very seldom any smaller or larger.
You'll need a float tube to fish it effectively, but you can drive right to it.
From Highway 50, take the paved Ice House Road (also marked Forest
Road 3), past Union Valley Reservoir. Keep left on Forest Road 30
(Loon Lake is to the right), cross Gerle Creek, then turn left into Gerle
Creek Campground. Drive round the loop road to the picnic area,
between campsites 30 and 31.

THE SOUTH FORK OF THE AMERICAN RIVER
DeLorme: p. 89, B3; p. 88, B7
USFS: Eldorado National Forest
USGS: Echo Lake, Pyramid Peak,
Kyburz, Riverton, Pollock Pines, Slate Mountain, Garden Valley
Altitude: 7400–2300 feet
Water types: Pools, riffles, runs, and pocket water.
Trout: Rainbows, 8–12 inches, plus some browns.

It's the South Fork of the American that you see when you're driving along Highway 50 to South Lake Tahoe. It has the worn look of most roadside streams, and you'd assume that it was heavily bait-fished and likely to contain planted trout. Both things are true, so I suspect fly fishers avoid it. Certainly I used to, until I fished above Kyburz, where the highway climbs above the river for the first time. The South Fork runs through a U-shaped canyon there, a hundred feet or so below the road, and angular rocks create pocket water and medium-depth runs. Wild rainbows aren't plentiful, but they're certainly pretty, with a pale pink stripe and purple parr marks above their bright orange fins. Downstream, where the river runs right next to the road, it's not to my taste, despite some tempting pools, since it's planted heavily. The South Fork leaves the highway again below Ice House Road, and there are wild trout, but it gets a bit warm by the late summer. The huge mud slides of 1997 dumped untold quantities of silt in the lower river, too, but it should have recovered by now.

Accesses are obvious, but you should know one thing. There are summer home tracts along here, and you might assume they would be private property. Well, they're not. These summer homes stand on national forest land, so you can fish through. Common courtesy still suggests that you shouldn't walk over somebody's front yard, however, or park in their driveway. Many roadside pullouts provide parking spots, as does the campground at Lovers Leap. Access to the lower river can be found at the Pacific House exit off Highway 50, where a dirt road marked "Dead End Road" leads 0.7 miles down to the river, or at Chili Bar on Highway 193 north from Placerville, below Chili Bar Reservoir.

STRAWBERRY CREEK
DeLorme: p. 89, C7–B6
USFS: Eldorado National Forest
USGS: Pyramid Peak
Altitude: 8800–5700 feet
Water types: Tiny pools and runs.
Trout: Browns, 8–10 inches; rainbows, 6–8 inches, plus
occasional brook trout.

This creek might seem too tiny to fish, but it runs through a long, shallow valley, providing steady runs and tree-root cover for brown trout. The gold-and-orange rocks shelter plenty of mayfly nymphs, too, a testament to the creek's fertility. In places, little meadows slope down among the red fir trees, so there are pale-blue hound's tongues, dark-blue delphiniums, and orange lilies to admire in the early summer. This stream isn't very suitable for the beginner, since the browns are spooky in the thin water, but upstream, where the gradient steepens, there is faster water that holds some little rainbows. Take Highway 50 to milepost 42 and turn right through the Strawberry Creek tract. Cross the South Fork of the American and in 0.4 miles go right to a bridge over Strawberry Creek, or stay left on Strawberry Creek Road, which parallels the creek for several miles and dead-ends where two tiny forks join to make up the creek.

THE SILVER FORK OF THE AMERICAN RIVER
DeLorme: p. 89, C6–B5
USFS: Eldorado National Forest
USGS: Tragedy Spring, Kyburz
Altitude: 7300–4100 feet
Water types: Pools, runs, and pocket water.
Trout: Rainbows, 7–12 inches; browns, 8–12 inches, some bigger,
plus occasional brook trout.

The Silver Fork leaves Silver Lake as a small tailwater, then flows over a series of granite benches from a hundred feet to half a mile wide. Small waterfalls empty into large pools there, which harbor some sizable browns. Then the stream tumbles steeply through short plunge pools to join its main tributary, Caples Creek, another small tailwater. Below Caples Creek, faster runs and pocket water hide wild rainbows until the first road bridge. It's a medium-sized stream by that point, and a paved road runs along it for several miles, giving access to two campgrounds. There are some nice pools there, and though they mostly hold planted rainbows, wild trout can still be found. However, this is a stream where hiking in is not only advisable, but easily done.

To reach the Silver Fork, turn right off Highway 50 at Kyburz onto Silver Fork Road. Keep left at the first junction and follow the paved road over the hill. It parallels the stream for about 6 miles before crossing it on a bridge just after Silver Fork Campground. You can fish upstream from the bridge, and the angling gradually will get better and better. Just before the bridge on the left, though, is an old jeep road. This leads to the well-maintained Caples Creek Trail, which heads upstream, then alongside Caples Creek for a while. Then it intersects with the Silver Fork Trail, which crosses Caples Creek on a footbridge, continues fairly steeply around the side of a bluff, and drops down to the Silver Fork on the largest of the benches. You could also access the upper reaches from Highway 88 at Silver Lake. There, the stream again sees quite a bit of fishing pressure, but browns seem to avoid bait much better than rainbows, so don't worry—there are wild trout. Once again, the farther you walk, the better, though you'll have to pick your way over big sheets of bare granite to get downstream. The other end of the trail (the Old Silver Lake Trail) is found at Martin Meadow, about a mile and a half northeast of Silver Lake, and leads to the Silver Fork in 2 miles.

CAPLES CREEK
DeLorme: p. 89, C7–C6
USFS: Eldorado National Forest
USGS: Caples Lake, Tragedy Spring
Altitude: 7900–5900 feet
Water types: Small pools, runs, and pocket water.
Trout: Rainbows, 7–10 inches; browns, 8–12 inches.

This tributary of the Silver Fork of the American offers similar fishing for wild fish. It drains Caples Lake, just a few miles farther up Highway 88 from Silver Lake. Near the lake, it's rather brushy and tough to fish, but downstream, where the Caples Creek Trail gives access, it's much easier fishing, though it's still not as open as the Silver Fork. Just above where it joins the Silver Fork, the trout are all browns, but they're mostly rainbows upstream of the footbridge. For trail access-es, see the Silver Fork of the American River listing above. The Caples Creek Trail parallels the creek for quite a ways, and the Old Silver Lake Trail joins the former if you wish to come from Highway 88. Start at Martin Meadows and keep right where the Silver Fork is to the left.

SILVER CREEK
DeLorme: p. 88, B4–B3
USFS: Eldorado National Forest
USGS: Riverton, Pollock Pines
Altitude: 4600–2600 feet
Water types: Open pools and runs.
Trout: Browns, 9–12 inches.

I have to admit, I've seldom fished here, despite reports of large browns. The reason will be clear if you've noticed how much time I spend discussing the nature of a fishery's surroundings, as opposed to the size of its trout. The main stem of this extensive drainage leaves Junction Reservoir in an ugly, despoiled canyon. This is not the natural order of things, but this little reservoir is far enough from anywhere for no one to notice what the dam has done to the stream. They must turn the flow right off for most of the year, then let a huge flood scour away all the gravel bars whenever they have to dump water in the spring. As a result, there are few trout, though I'll admit they're quite large for a small stream. Even worse, it requires a rather unsafe climb down a loose scree slope to get there. If you must go, take Ice House Road from Highway 50, then turn left onto Forest Road 31 (stay right at the fork). After 5.4 miles on Forest Road 31, take the gravel road on the left, which leads around the south shore of the reservoir to a parking area below the dam. Watch the climb!

THE SOUTH FORK OF SILVER CREEK
DeLorme: p. 89, B6; p. 88, B4
USFS: Eldorado National Forest
USGS: Kyburz, Riverton
Altitude: 8200–4600 feet
Water types: Small pools, runs, and pocket water.
Trout: Rainbows, 6–10 inches; browns, 9–12 inches.

This stream is positively schizophrenic. Above Ice House Reservoir, it trickles over great sheets of pale granite in a wide channel surrounded by heavy forest, while below the reservoir, it pushes strongly through pocket water surrounded by dark rocks, while the hills on either side of the canyon are almost bare. It will surprise no one that the dam is responsible for the huge difference in flow, while a recent wildfire caused the open hills. Much of the land below the dam is private, so study the Forest Service map carefully. It offers quite good fishing in the little canyon below Silver Creek Campground, just upstream of the burn zone, and there are brown trout there. Above Ice House Reservoir, the trout are mostly little rainbows, but this open stream would be a good place for beginners from the early summer on into midsummer, before the flow gets too low.

Take Ice House Road from Highway 50. Silver Creek Campground is on the left in about 9 miles, just before the bridge over the South Fork of Silver Creek. For the upper reaches, turn right on Forest Road 32 to Ice House Reservoir. In 3.8 miles, take road 12N25 to the right. In 0.5 miles, go straight ahead onto a dirt road, then stay left at the fork. The road ends beside the creek in a mile. This is only one of several possible accesses.

Don't bother with some of the other creeks in this area. **Big Silver Creek** is rather misnamed, since both it and its tributary, the **Bassi Fork,** drop to a trickle by the late summer. Small rainbows are there, though, and even a few smallmouth bass, in the pools just above Union Valley Reservoir. The **Jones Fork of Silver Creek** dries up almost completely.

SLAB CREEK
DeLorme: p. 88, B3/2
USFS: Eldorado National Forest
USGS: Slate Mountain
Altitude: 4600–2000 feet
Water types: Little pools and runs.
Trout: Rainbows, 6–10 inches; browns, 8–11 inches.

Slab Creek is pleasant, for something so comparatively near to civilization. It runs through old-growth fir and incense cedar forest, burbling between mossy rocks below a canopy of maples, dogwoods, and (a touch of personal nostalgia for this transplanted native of the old country), yew trees! It may be spring-fed, because it still flows quite well through the fall, and both mayflies and caddisflies are quite prolific. There was evidence of bait-fishing pressure when I fished it, though, which may account for trout being plentiful in May and conspicuous by their absence in October. It's not easy to fish, for the going is rough in the narrow canyon, and overhanging branches obstruct your casting, but that's a welcome challenge for the true small-stream enthusiast.

From Georgetown, on Highway 193, head northeast on Main Street, which becomes Wentworth Springs Road. In 10.8 miles, just past Quintette, turn right on Sand Mountain Road (Forest Road 13). In 4.6 miles, stay right at a fork, and the pavement turns to well-graded dirt. In another half of a mile, turn left, back onto a paved road signposted to Slab Creek. The bridge over the creek is 3.2 miles. There would be other accesses upstream, but it's private property. A tough hike in at some point downstream might be rewarding.

ROCK CREEK
DeLorme: p. 88, A1–B1
USFS: Eldorado National Forest
USGS: Tunnel Hill, Slate Mountain, Garden Valley.
Altitude: 3300–1300 feet
Water types: Little pools and runs.
Trout: Rainbows, 6–9 inches.

Rock Creek wouldn't make it onto anyone's list of the top 10 trout streams of the Sierra. In fact, it might not make the top 200 on mine. But this is a low-elevation trout stream, and precious enough by virtue of its rarity. It should be fished only in the early season, before it drops to a trickle, and then only if you can stand some clambering. The canyon is pretty enough to make it worth the steep hike, but make sure the fly rod you take is a tiny one so you don't feel too annoyed about carrying it. There are little trout beneath the live oaks and Douglas-fir-clad slopes, and sometimes that's enough, when raging snowmelt keeps you from fishing the higher elevations.

The trails into the canyon are numerous, and they're listed on the Hiking Trails of the Sierra leaflet, obtainable from the Eldorado National Forest at the address and phone number listed in the "Maps" section of "How to Get There, Stay There, and Stay Safe" above. From Georgetown, on Highway 193, take Wentworth Springs Road 5.9 miles to Balderston and turn right onto Balderston Road, then left on Mace Mill Road in 0.9 miles, or continue another 0.9 miles to a left on Darling Ridge Road. The roads are paved, but four-wheel-drive tracks lead to some of the trails.

LODGING NEAR THE AMERICAN RIVER, NORTH AND MIDDLE FORKS

There are no lodgings very close to any of the fisheries on the North and Middle Forks of the American, but these small towns offer some nice old inns and bed and breakfasts, while chain motels can be found in Auburn, on Interstate 80.

Coloma

Coloma Country Inn
Bed and breakfast
(530) 622-6919

Golden Lotus
Bed and breakfast inn and
restaurant
(530) 621-4562

Georgetown

American River Inn
Historic hotel
1-800-245-6566

Foresthill

Forest House
Historic inn and restaurant
(530) 367-2840

Auburn

Auburn InnMotel
1-800-272-1444

Best WesternMotel
1-800-201-0121

Elmwood Motel
(530) 885-5186
Foothills Motel
(530) 885-8444

Holiday Inn Motel
1-800-814-8787

Sleep Inn Motel
(530) 888-7829

Super 8 Motel
1-800-848-8888

Travelodge Motel
(530) 885-7025

Powers Mansion Inn
Bed and breakfast
(530) 885-1166

Loomis
Emma's Bed and Breakfast
(530) 652-1392

Old Flower Farm Inn
Bed and breakfast
(530) 652-4200

CAMPSITES

These are all National Forest Service campgrounds. Those that charge a fee are operated by concessionaires and cost an average of $10 per site. Sites at those marked with the telephone icon ☎ can be reserved by calling 1-800-280-CAMP.

**Off Interstate 80
(the North Fork of the North Fork)**

North Fork
Exit Interstate 80 at Emigrant Gap
Fee, piped water

Foresthill Road (the North Fork)

Giant Gap ☎
Sugar Pine Reservoir
Fee, piped water

Shirttail Creek ☎
Sugar Pine Reservoir
Fee, piped water

Big Reservoir
Off Foresthill Road
Fee, piped water

Secret House
Foresthill Road
No fee, no water

Robinson Flat
Foresthill Road
No fee, well water

**French Meadows
(the Upper Middle Fork)**

French Meadows ☎
South shore of reservoir
Fee, piped water

Lewis ☎
North shore of reservoir
Fee, piped water

Poppy
Accessible by boat or trail only
No fee, no water

Ahart
1 mile east of reservoir
Fee, piped water

Talbot
5 miles east of reservoir
No fee, no water

The Upper Rubicon

Big Meadows
Northwest of reservoir
Fee, piped water

Hell Hole
Northwest of reservoir
Fee, piped water

Upper Hell Hole
Accessible by boat or trail only
No fee, no water

The Middle Rubicon

Stumpy Meadows ☎
Wentworth Springs Road
Fee, piped water

You will find a few rough camping spots in the Tahoe and Eldorado National Forests in this area.

Lodging Near the South Fork American River

Most of these lodgings aren't particularly close to the fisheries in the area of the South Fork, but there are some nice old inns and bed and breakfasts, and plenty of restaurants in Placerville.

Coloma

Coloma Country Inn
Bed and breakfast
(530) 622-6919

Golden Lotus
Bed and breakfast
Inn and restaurant
(530) 621-4562

Georgetown

American River Inn
Historic hotel
1-800-245-6566

Placerville

Best Western InnMotel
1-800-528-1234

Cary House Hotel
Historic hotel
(530) 622-4271

Chichester McKee House
Bed and breakfast
(530) 626-1882

Garden Gate Inn
Bed and breakfast
(530) 621-4068

Mother Lode Motel
(530) 622-0895

National 9 Inn
Motel
(530) 622-3884

Seasons
Bed and Breakfast
Rooms and cabins
(530) 626-4420

Shadowridge Ranch
Cabins
(530) 295-1000

Shafsky House
Bed and breakfast
(530) 642-2776

In Camino (Highway 50)

Camino Hotel
1-800-200-7740

In Pollock Pines (Highway 50)

Stagecoach Inn
Motel
(530) 644-2029

Near Kyburz

Strawberry Lodge
Rooms
(530) 659-7200

Near Silver Lake on Highway 88

Kit Carson Lodge
Motel rooms and cottages
(209) 258-8500

Campsites

All are National Forest Service campgrounds unless otherwise stated. Those that charge a fee are operated by concessionaires and cost an average of $10 per site. Sites at those marked the telephone icon ☎ can be reserved by calling 1-800-280-CAMP.

Ice House Road

Wrights Lake ☎
On Wrights Lake
Fee, piped water

Ice House Resort
Ice House Road
Private camp, fee,
showers, groceries

Strawberry Point
On Ice House Reservoir
Fee, no water

Northwind
On Ice House Reservoir
No fee, no water

Ice House ☎
On Ice House Reservoir
Fee, piped water

Silver Creek
On South Fork Silver Creek
Fee, no water

Fashoda
Walk-in
On Union Valley Reservoir
Fee, piped water

Jones Fork
On Union Valley Reservoir
Fee, no water

Sunset ☎
On Union Valley Reservoir
Fee, piped water

Wench Creek
On Union Valley Reservoir
Fee, piped water

Wolf Creek ☎
On Union Valley Reservoir
No fee, no water

Yellowjacket ☎
On Union Valley Reservoir
Fee, piped water

South Fork
On South Fork Rubicon
Fee, no water

Airport Flat
On Gerle Creek
No fee, no water

Gerle Creek ☎
On Gerle Creek Reservoir
Fee, piped water

Wentworth Springs
Accessible only by jeep road
No fee, no water

Loon Lake ☎
On Loon Lake
Fee, piped water

Northshore
On Loon Lake
No fee, no water

Highway 50 / Silver Fork Road

Sand Flat
Just off Highway 50
Fee, piped water

China Flat
On the Silver Fork American
Fee, piped water

Silver Fork
On Silver Fork American
Fee, piped water

Lovers Leap
Just off Highway 50
Fee, piped water

Highway 88

Silver Lake East ☎
On Silver Lake
Fee, piped water

Silver Lake West
On Silver Lake
Fee, piped water

Kirkwood
On Upper Caples Creek
Fee, piped water

Caples Lake
On Caples Lake
Fee, piped water

You will find quite a few rough camping spots in the Eldorado National Forest.

SUPPLIES

Anglers fishing the North or Middle Forks of the American can obtain groceries and camping supplies in Auburn or Foresthill. There are plenty of restaurants and a brew pub in Auburn.

Anglers fishing the South Fork of the American can obtain groceries and camping supplies in Georgetown or Placerville, or at the Ice House Resort or Robb's Valley Resort on Ice House Road. Robb's Valley Resort sells propane and gas, and the bar and restaurant there offers hot meals. The wonderfully funky building was built by the owner and his son from felled trees, cut by hand. Hot showers are available there, too, for a modest fee. Check it out.

FLY-FISHING SUPPLIES

The American Fly Fishing Co.
3523 Fair Oaks Boulevard
Sacramento, CA 95864
(916) 483-1222
Web site: www.americanfly.com
A full-service fly shop close to Highway 50 at Lott Avenue.

Fly Fishing Specialties
6412 Tupelo Drive
Sacramento, CA 95621
(916) 722-1055
A full-service fly shop just off Interstate 80 at the Antelope exit.

Kiene's Fly Shop
2654 Marconi Avenue
Sacramento, CA 95821
(916) 486-9958
Web site: www.kiene.com
A full-service fly shop northeast of downtown. Take the Marconi Avenue exit off Interstate 80.

Chapter 8: The Carson River Area

Like the Truckee, the Carson River drains eastward, and the terrain of its forks and tributaries is rugged and stark, with an aridity that hints at the desert land of its destination, the Great Basin of Nevada. Here there may well be scorpions, for all I know. The countryside is handsome, though, with its red-rock canyons, spreading alpine meadows, and aspen groves. It's lightly visited, and Alpine County is the least-densely populated county in all of California. It's almost as if you have stepped back several decades to a slower, quieter time, when the state wasn't quite the bustling economic engine that it is today. Which is just the thing a fly fisher seeks . . . along with large rainbow, brown, or cutthroat trout. There's a chance that you'll find all of these here. Just watch where you step. Scorpions, you know. And rattlers, and. . . .

East Fork of the Carson River, Grays Crossing. Here you'll find wild browns and rainbows.

THE EAST FORK OF THE CARSON RIVER

DeLorme: p. 90, D3–B3
USFS: Toiyabe National Forest
USGS: Wolf Creek, Heenan Lake, Markleeville, Carter Station
Altitude: 7000–5200 feet
Water types: A meadow stream, then riffles and pools, with some pocket water.
Trout: Rainbows, 9–20 inches; browns, 12–20 inches, plus a few cutthroats and brook trout.
Special Regulations: Above Carson Falls, closed to all fishing. From Hangmans Bridge to the Nevada State Line, zero trout, artificial lures with barbless hooks only.

The East Fork of the Carson can break your heart. It's the lover you'll wish you'd never met. You'll get skunked—I know it'll happen—but you'll come back for more, I can guarantee that, too. Department of Fish and Game surveys show that it has far fewer trout per mile than any of the other east-slope waters in the Wild Trout Program. If you catch a fish in the special regulations section, it's almost as likely to be 18 inches long as it is to be 8. But study the "If" at the beginning of the last sentence again and make sure that you take it in. Local guide Jim Crouse tabulates the surveys that anglers fill out, and in 1998, they averaged 0.65 trout per hour, mostly rainbows from 10 to 14 inches, with a few in the 18-to-20-inch range. On top of that, Jim also estimates that three-quarters of those who got skunked didn't bother to fill out a survey. The low trout numbers appear to be caused by poor spawning success, and the Department of Fish and Game is still studying the reasons at the time of this writing. The East Fork is also one of the last streams to come into fishable shape, since the volcanic silt from spring runoff doesn't settle out until mid-July in most years, which may also contribute to the low spawning success.

The East Fork is one of the very few free-flowing rivers in the Sierra, flowing unimpeded by dams for 70 miles to Lahontan Reservoir, deep into Nevada. It rises in the Carson-Iceberg Wilderness at almost ten thousand feet, but we don't have to examine the first 12 miles of its flow, since we can't fish there. The river is closed above Carson Falls to protect the native Lahontan cutthroats that have been reestablished above that natural barrier. Below the falls, the next 16 miles are designated as a Wild Trout fishery for rainbows, brookies, and browns, though

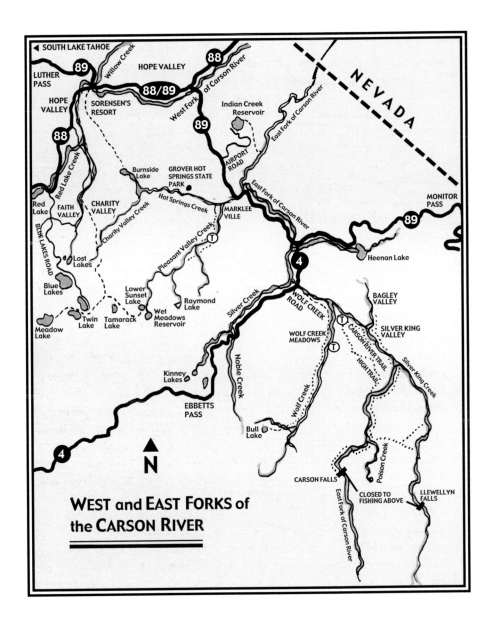

WEST and EAST FORKS of the CARSON RIVER

with the regular five-fish limit. The river runs through typical east-slope terrain, dry pine woods alternating with sagebrush-covered slopes and several named meadows, all a long way from any road. The first is Falls Meadow, then Dumonts Meadow, where the Forest Service maintains the Soda Springs Guard Station. Finally, the river turns to the north again to flow through the lovely, wide-open meadows of Silver King Valley, the first place that the river comes within a viable day hike.

Below Silver King Valley, the canyon narrows again, and the river runs beneath towering spires and fluted castellations of volcanic rock decorated with orange lichen. The Carson River Trail gives access here, though it's often high above the river. Cottonwoods and willows line the banks, while the river adopts a pool-and-riffle structure all the way to the junction with Wolf Creek, where you'll find the first road access. The canyon becomes steeper then, and the pools bigger, as the East Fork starts to hurry toward Nevada. Just below the Silver Creek confluence, the river reaches a paved road for the first time, and it's here, along Highway 4, that heavy fishing pressure and planted trout become a feature.

At Hangmans Bridge, just south of the small town of Markleeville, the next Wild Trout section of the river begins, this time with the special regulations listed above. Here, the East Fork leaves the company of the highway again as far as the Nevada state line and beyond. The river flows through true high desert, meandering past cliffs of volcanic rock in shades of purplish-brown, deep pink, and yellow-ocher. The hills above the river are sparsely covered with dark, blackish-green junipers and occasional piñon pines, while the brighter greens of cottonwoods, aspens, or willows are seen only in the narrow riparian zone along the river. Access is again by trail, though some people float this lower section in rafts, camping as they go.

The fishing on the East Fork can be divided into three distinct sections. The upper river varies quite a bit, from an open meadow stream with some undercut banks to long stretches with shallow riffles, runs, and a few rocky pools. The trout are all wild, and the fishing isn't particularly difficult. If you decide to backpack in, the better fishing is above Soda Springs Guard Station, rather than in the first few miles downstream of it. These meadows are still recovering from overgrazing in the past, so the fishing will continue to get better. In a 1996 Department of Fish and Game survey, lots of brook trout were found above Poison Creek. Rainbow trout, usually no bigger than 14 inches, hold in the open pools and runs in Silver King Valley and through the canyon below. Bank undercuts or tree roots provide cover for the less common brown trout, which can get a little bigger and sport a healthy blue-green iridescence on their sides. General dries like the Humpy, the Parachute or standard Adams, and the Elk Hair Caddis make good searching patterns, while a hopper pattern is always worth a try in the meadow sections, since they crawl with grasshoppers in the summer. Nymph fishing is effective, too, of course, but much of the water is better suited to exploring with a dry fly.

The middle section of the river, alongside Highways 4 and 89, has deeper pools and some larger fish, though many of them will be planted. Alpine County is well aware that it makes most of its living as a tourist destination, so the chamber of commerce plants many trout in the county's streams. They're often much larger than Fish and Game's planters, running to as much as four pounds. Big Lahontan cutthroats may be caught here, as well, large brood-stock fish that Fish and Game traps from Heenan Lake for its spawning program, then releases in the East Fork. There are wild fish, too, though, both rainbows and browns, but the bait-fishing pressure can be considerable. Here, nymph fishing comes into its own, as does streamer fishing. Try beadhead patterns under an indicator, or fish Woolly Buggers deep and slow. For dries, the same patterns recommended for the upper river will work, but consider carrying the more exact imitations you will need for the fussier fish of the lower river, as well.

In the lower Wild Trout section, fish can be few and far between, but they're often large, and mainly rainbows. I have to be honest and admit that I've never done well here, but I know many people who have. Look over Hangmans Bridge on an average weekend and you'll probably see several fly fishers spread out downstream, though the fishing can be better below the junction with Markleeville Creek, about a mile away. Nymph fishing is a must, unless you see fish rising, but the evening hatch can help you locate those sparse fish populations. Fishable water is well spread out, too, since long stretches of unproductive shallows separate the good pools from each other. A lot of walking can be required, so carry plenty of water. In the large pools there, more exact dry-fly patterns become important during hatches, so try parachute or comparadun mayfly imitations or caddis emergers that fish in the film.

The hatches of the East Carson are hard to tabulate, because the varied topography supports so many different aquatic insects. However, mayflies and caddises predominate in the upper river, while stoneflies

become more common in the middle reaches. Golden Stones hatch in July
and August, along with *Rhyacophila* and *Hydropsyche* caddises. Hoppers
and ant patterns can be very useful in the afternoons during the midsummer. In the fall, the *Baetis* hatch prolifically, along with several other
small mayflies, which makes it a particularly good time for dry-fly fishing. October Caddises may be present then, too, and these large, orange-
bodied insects are certainly worth imitating if you see them. Jim Crouse
tells me this hatch can start as early as Labor Day or not happen until
November, and this variability is something that's true of most of the
Carson River's hatches.

EAST FORK OF THE CARSON HATCH TABLE

Insect	Dates	Size
Pale Evening Duns (various)	July–September	16–20
Pale Morning Duns (*Ephemerella infrequens, inermis*)	July–September	16–18
Tricos	August	20–22
Blue-Winged Olive (*Baetis*)	mid-September–November	18–20
Spotted Sedge (*Hydropsyche*)	June– September	12–14
Green Sedge (*Rhyacophila*)	June–October	10–14
Grannom (*Brachycentrus*)	July–August	14–16
Saddle-Case Caddis (*Glossosoma*)	mid-July-September	16–18
October Caddis (*Dicosmoecus*)	mid-September–November	6–8
Golden Stonefly (*Calineuria*)	May–mid-July	6–10
Little Yellow Stonefly (*Isoperla*)	June–August	14–18
Midges	All Season	20-24

This hatch table is equally valid for the West Fork of the Carson. There are other early season hatches, for instance Salmon Flies, but they all come during runoff.

To reach the upper section of the East Fork of the Carson, take Highway 89 south from Markleeville, stay on Highway 4 where 89 and 4 divide, then turn left, signposted to Wolf Creek Meadows. The road crosses Silver Creek and gives access to the river for half a mile, then it becomes dirt and climbs a ridge before dropping down into Wolf Creek Meadows in 3.3 miles. Take the first left, signposted to the Carson River and the High Trail. You'll cross Wolf Creek, then turn right to the trailhead. From there the Carson River Trail heads uphill, and in a few hundred yards you'll come to the junction with the High Trail. The High Trail is only for those intending to stay overnight in the Carson-Iceberg Wilderness, since it climbs over the ridge top and doesn't approach the river for almost 7 miles, in Dumonts Meadows.

On the Carson River Trail, you'll climb a ridge to a gate, then drop down to grassy little Wolf Creek Lake in about a mile. In a quarter of a mile, you'll come to a fork where Gray's Crossing is signposted to the left. This trail leads you down to the river after another mile, arriving at a shallow ford. The old river trail used to cross the ford and route itself up Bagley Valley a short distance before heading south into Silver King Valley. It's probably still the shortest route to that point. If you branch right back at the fork, the new Carson River Trail stays well above the river, but there are some gentle slopes you could make your way down. It's a total distance of 5 miles from the trailhead to Silver King Valley, though you'll reach river level half a mile before the meadow.

If you're not keen on the hiking, there is access to the river back at Wolf Creek. Instead of turning right to the trailhead, stay left on the dirt road, which winds down onto a bluff above the East Fork. Steep paths lead down the slope on your right to the river, but the easiest access is to your left, near the point of the bluff, where a trail slopes gently down the side of the shallow Wolf Creek canyon to the confluence of the two streams. The East Fork's canyon is quite wide here, so it's easy to make your way upstream or downstream. A mile upstream, the canyon narrows, but you'll still find trails along the bank, and some slightly better pools, as well.

Access to the middle and lower river is easy. Take Highway 89 south from Markleeville and you'll come to Hangmans Bridge in 2 miles.

Highways 89 and then 4 run alongside the river for 5 miles. You can hike downstream from Hangmans Bridge along the north bank, but there is a gated dirt road above the river on the south side that gives easier access. Park in the pullout on the left, on the south of the bridge, and climb the gate. The road leads downstream for almost 3 miles, then a trail continues beyond that.

SILVER KING CREEK
DeLorme: p. 100, A4; p. 90, D4
USFS: Toiyabe National Forest
USGS: Lost Cannon Peak, Coleville
Altitude: 8000–6400 feet
Water types: Small pools and runs, then a meadow stream.
Trout: Rainbows, 8–12 inches.
Special Regulations: Closed to all fishing above Llewellyn Falls.

Silver King Creek is not going to be visited by the casual angler, since its drainage is entirely within the Carson-Iceberg Wilderness. It's also the last refuge of a beautiful and rare trout, the Paiute cutthroat, which is why it's closed to all fishing above Llewellyn Falls. The adventurous can reach this stream with a strenuous hike, though, and find abundant, colorful, rainbows of some size in wild country. It has been proposed that the Department of Fish and Game treat the stream below the falls and reintroduce Paiute cutthroats, so it's possible that catch-and-release angling for these rare trout will be allowed in the future.

The upstream access is from the trailheads at Rodriguez Flat or Little Antelope Pack Station. To get there, you have to take Highway 395, either heading south from Monitor Pass or north from Highway 108 (Sonora Pass). You turn west onto Mill Canyon Road between the small towns of Walker and Coleville, then keep right on Golden Canyon Road, which leads to the trailhead in 6.3 miles. From there, you could reach the stream via either the Snodgrass Creek Trail or the Driveway Trail, neither of which I have hiked. You'll need a topo map or the Carson-Iceberg Wilderness Guide, by Jeffrey Schaffer, published by Wilderness Press. This book comes with a separate 1:62,500 map. The contour intervals are 80 feet on this useful map, which marks trails very clearly. From Little Antelope Pack Station, you could get horse-packed in, too. (See "Services" below.)

The downstream access is in Silver King Valley, reached by a 5-mile hike on the Carson River Trail, described under the East Fork of the Carson River listing. Wade across the East Fork and hike less than a mile southeast, to where Silver King Creek runs through the meadows to join the East Fork.

WOLF CREEK
DeLorme: p. 90, D3
USFS: Toiyabe National Forest
USGS: Wolf Creek
Altitude: 8200–6300 feet
Water types: Fast runs and riffles, then a small meadow stream.
Trout: Rainbows, 8–11 inches; brook trout, 7–10 inches; browns, 9–12 inches.

This is a small, fast-flowing trout stream, accessible upstream for 5 miles by an easy trail that climbs so slowly that much of it seems almost level. It flows through a broad flood plain at the bottom of its gently sloping canyon and is filled with medium-sized cobble that is easily rearranged by floods. The heavy snowmelt in 1997 caused by warm spring rains flattened out much of the holding water, but trout populations should bounce back. The stream exits the Carson-Iceberg Wilderness and flows into Wolf Creek Meadows, a broad and very damp irrigated cow pasture. Then it exits the valley through a short, narrow canyon to its confluence with the East Fork. The upper reaches contain reasonable numbers of sizable rainbows, while brook trout get more abundant the farther you hike. Chunky browns may be encountered, too, particularly in the meadows, where undercuts give them cover. Just be careful of the bulls that graze among the cows and respect the private property by not climbing any fences.

To get there, turn left off Highway 4 onto Wolf Creek Road just after you cross the East Fork of the Carson and drive 3.3 miles to the meadows. If you continue to the end of the valley, you'll come to an unimproved campground and trailhead. Although the upper reaches are in the Carson-Iceberg Wilderness, you don't need a permit for day use. There is a self-service permit station, though, if you intend to stay overnight. The trail is mostly parallel to the creek for 6 miles upstream.

SILVER CREEK
DeLorme: p. 90, D2–D3
USFS: Toiyabe National Forest
USGS: Ebbetts Pass, Wolf Creek
Altitude: 6800–6000 feet
Water types: Small pools, runs, and pocket water.
Trout: Rainbows, 7–12 inches.

Silver Creek is a popular fishing spot, since it's paralleled by Highway 4 for most of its length. It's a pretty and prolific stream, though, with plenty of wild trout, all rainbows. It starts with several precipitous tributaries pouring down from dramatic high-mountain terrain around Ebbetts Pass. They join to form a viable fishery just below Silver Creek Campground. The canyon is steep-sided, and lined with a fascinating variety of rocks in every color, from blue-gray through green and red to purple. Beneath the crystal-clear water, the cobble that lines the streambed has the look of a giant jar of sugared almonds.

The native trout are equally beautifully colored, with a double row of faint purple-gray parr marks, white tips on their fins, a gold glow to their sides, and a faint orange shading on their bellies. However, you're also likely to catch planted rainbows, often large ones to as much as 14 inches. It would be hard to imagine a better, more poignant example of the difference between wild and planted fish, both in appearance and in behavior. The wild fish are skittish, needing to be approached cautiously with a small dry fly. Slap a large Elk Hair Caddis down hard, though, and a pewter-gray planter will charge six feet to eat it, then wallow about on the end of your leader as though confused. Eat a couple, if you like. There's no sense in letting the crop rot in the field!

Directions are unnecessary. Park along Highway 4 anywhere that the clamber down the slope from the road isn't too steep and fish upstream. **Noble Creek** is the main tributary to Silver Creek, and there's a hiking trail up its canyon, but I found it devoid of trout in 1997, though it's supposed to contain brookies.

Pleasant Valley Creek. A catch-and-release fee fishery that offers great scenery and large trout in close quarters.

PLEASANT VALLEY CREEK
DeLorme: p. 90, C2/D2
USFS: Toiyabe National Forest
USGS: Markleeville
Altitude: 6400–5700 feet
Water types: A meadow stream, but also pools, runs, and pocket water.
Trout: Wild rainbows, 9–14 inches, plus larger planted rainbows and some browns.
Special Regulations: Catch-and-release, artificial flies with barbless hooks only.

Until recently, Pleasant Valley Creek was open to the public, although it ran through private land. But in 1998, the owner finally decided he'd had enough of the many abuses of his property and closed the valley to public fishing. Now you can fish only in the Pleasant Valley Flyfishing Preserve by obtaining a permit through a licensed guide, Jim Crouse of

Alpine Fly Fishing. The cost is quite reasonable for private water, and you don't have to book guide services to fish it. Jim can be contacted at (530) 542-0759. There's only a very short section of the creek running through national forest land downstream of the valley that's open to the public.

Pleasant Valley richly deserves its name. As the well-graded dirt road drops down over the ridge and you get your first look at the surroundings, you're going to be impressed. A golden-colored peak resembling a Disneyland castle, with turrets and battlements of bare rock, towers above the valley to the west, while other spectacular peaks hem it in on every side. From these mountains, several small tributaries fall steeply, meeting in dense forest at the southwest end of the valley to form the creek. Open pine woods, then sagebrush and sloping meadows lead down to the meandering stream. It flows a bit too fast to have a stable channel, though you can find the occasional undercut bank or deep pool.

The stream exits the valley in a shallow, V-shaped canyon where pines, aspens, and wild roses cloak the banks and larger boulders provide pools and pocket water. This rougher water offers good fishing, since it's slightly easier to sneak up on the fish. The long stretch through the meadows provides challenging fishing and can be best during the evening mayfly hatches. It used to be heavily planted by both the Department of Fish and Game and Alpine County, but since 1998, only the landowner has introduced any trout. With catch-and-release regulations, the wild trout should increase and render planting largely unnecessary.

To get to Pleasant Valley Creek, turn right in the center of Markleeville onto Hot Springs Road, then turn left to Pleasant Valley in 1 mile. Park in the camping area on the left when you first reach the valley floor. Downstream is national forest land for a quarter of a mile or so. A hiking trail goes upstream through the valley on the northwest side, enters the pine woods, and crosses the stream in about a mile, near the top of the valley. However, it doesn't enter national forest land until it has climbed many hundreds of feet above the creek, so it would be difficult to use it to access the public fishing. I recommend buying a day permit to fish in the valley, particularly if the brown trout make a comeback. Back in the 1930s and 1940s, when Fish and Game rented the ranch to operate a hatchery, very large browns were taken from this creek, and private catch-and-release fishing may yet restore them.

CHARITY VALLEY CREEK
DeLorme: p. 90, C1
USFS: Toiyabe National Forest
USGS: Carson Pass
Altitude: 7800–7200 feet
Water types: A tiny meadow stream, then pools and runs.
Trout: Brook trout, 6–9 inches.

Charity Valley Creek is a tiny meadow stream with plenty of brook trout that don't get very big. Cattle graze this rather lovely high alpine meadow down to the banks, but it's a private inholding within the national forest that isn't fenced against access, so it would be churlish to complain. Follow it downstream, or even better, take the Charity Valley Trail, and you'll find some little, ungrazed meadows and tiny pools and runs.

You get there by turning off Highway 88 south onto Blue Lakes Road. You'll see the trail marked just before you come to the meadow, about 6 miles from Highway 88.

HOT SPRINGS CREEK
DeLorme: p. 90, C1/2
USFS: Toiyabe National Forest
USGS: Markleeville
Altitude: 7800–5700 feet
Water types: Tiny pools and runs.
Trout: Rainbows, 6–10 inches.

This creek drains Burnside Lake, joins Charity Valley Creek, and falls steeply into another lovely valley. It's the site of Grover Hot Springs State Park, which has not only some well-visited hot springs, but a large, luxurious campground. The lower reaches of the stream see quite a bit of fishing pressure and get their fair share of planters, considering how tiny the stream is. I would recommend fishing it only if you were actually camping there, to get a hot shower. Then I'd hike the trail from the overflow parking area upstream and fish above the meadows, where a few wild rainbows can be caught. Hot Springs Creek below the state park seems rather slow, silty, and lacking in good trout habitat.

Spratt Creek is a tiny tributary with even tinier trout. I went there so that you wouldn't have to.

HEENAN LAKE
DeLorme: p. 90, C3
USFS: Toiyabe National Forest
USGS: Heenan Lake
Altitude: 7100 feet
Trout: Lahontan cutthroats.
Special Regulations: Catch-and-release fishing with artificial lures with bar-
bless hooks only, and only on Fridays, Saturdays, and Sundays from the
Friday before Labor Day through the last Sunday in October. No fishing
after sunset.

A very fertile, 130-acre reservoir, this is one of California's few
Wild Trout Lakes. The Department of Fish and Game uses it as a
brood-stock lake for Lahontan cutthroats, and it's open for only a brief
period of catch-and-release fishing in the fall. The words "brood stock"
might conjure up pictures of the ugly, black, tailless rainbows sometimes cleared out of hatcheries and dumped in streams, but nothing
could be further from the truth. There are two strains of cutthroat trout
here, the pure-strain Independence Lake fish, which have their adipose
fins clipped, and a remnant population of Carson drainage cutthroats that
are slightly interbred with rainbows. The trout are trapped each spring,
when they run up Heenan Creek to spawn, then fin-clipped adults are
selected for stripping of their eggs and milt. Their pure-strain progeny
go back into the lake as fingerlings. The first cast I ever made here, I
hooked a 20-inch cutthroat that was as deep in the body as a jack
salmon, with a broad wrist to its tail, translucent gold fins, delicate pink
sides with just a few spots, and a bluish-olive back. These beautiful
trout have bounced back strongly from a die-off that caused a brief closure in 1993.

Wooded hills rise above Heenan Lake on the northeast side, while
aspens grow in a few draws in the bare slopes to the southeast. The
land at the south end of the lake is open and gives spectacular views down
Bagley Valley to the distant peaks of the Carson-Iceberg Wilderness. The
lake's water is a rich soup of olive-green algae by fall, contrasting with the
dried brown grass around it. The only shade is provided by a few Jeffrey
pines and junipers.

Like Martis Creek Reservoir, it has a population of blood midges.
These midges are thought of as a summer hatch, but there are actually

several subspecies, some of which hatch in the fall. One of these is a huge dark-olive midge, almost a size 10! The conventional wisdom is that a large Prince Nymph is the best pattern here, because the cutthroats are rumored to be unselective. Well, what do you think that Prince Nymph looks like? Midge pupae are active deep in the water for a while before they rise to the surface to hatch. Try some large midge pupa patterns in brown, claret, or olive on a sinking line. All the typical lake insects are abundant, too, such as *Callibaetis* mayflies, caddises, scuds, and smaller midges. Streamers like Woolly Buggers may be the best way to catch a really big trout, though, and they can get to 26 inches, maybe even larger.

To get to the lake, take Highway 89 south from Markleeville and stay on Highway 89 to Monitor Pass when Highway 4 splits off. A dirt road leading into the parking area will be on your right in 3.7 miles, shortly after you see the dam. You could launch a pram if you hauled it down the steep, rocky slope to the lake (electric motors only), but float tubes and pontoon boats are a little more practical. Remember that you have to be off the lake by sunset, and note that the warden locks the gate of the parking lot park at dusk. Expect crowds, because this is a popular fishery.

BULL LAKE
DeLorme: p. 90, D2
USFS: Toiyabe National Forest
USGS: Wolf Creek (for the trail), Ebbetts Pass (for the lake)
Altitude: 7100 feet
Trout: Lahontan cutthroats.

This lake is a long way from anywhere, but may still be of interest to the backpacker. I have been there and out in a day, but though it wasn't completely exhausting, the 7-mile hike each way didn't leave a lot of fishing time. This lake is special, though, being one of the very few with a self-sustaining population of Lahontan cutthroats. It was chemically treated many years ago, and rare Paiute cutthroats were introduced. When the Department of Fish and Game surveyed the lake several years later, not a Paiute could be found, but heavily spotted Lahontan cutts were plentiful. They still aren't sure how they survived the rotenone and are about to test them genetically to see how pure they are. If they're reasonably pure, this lake will get special regulations and may even be limited to catch-

and-release angling. Ten years ago, the trout were both big and plentiful, but they aren't today, and this little lake shows signs of a lot of use by horse packers. Let's hope that it gets some protection soon.

It's a pretty lake, as well, closely surrounded by wooded slopes on two sides, while on the north and west, feeder streams tumble in through small, sloping meadows. These banks provide the most fly-casting room. The outflow stream is unusual in that it runs fairly level for some distance, providing more spawning territory. It seems to be fertile, and the inflow streams bring strange hatches like the large mayfly duns the trout were eating when I was there.

To get there, take the Wolf Creek Trail (see the Wolf Creek listing) 4.8 miles to a junction where you turn right, signposted to Bull Canyon. This junction is half a mile after you go through a gate, then pass close to the base of a steep cliff. The Bull Canyon Trail climbs steeply for 1.5 miles, then crosses Bull Creek. You climb along a broad ridge with a small, sloping meadow on your left. At the top of the meadow is a T junction, and the lake is to the left, a quarter of a mile or so.

BURNSIDE LAKE
DeLorme: p. 90, C1
USFS: Toiyabe National Forest
USGS: Markleeville
Altitude: 8200 feet
Trout: Planted rainbows.

Burnside Lake is a popular drive-to lake with plenty of bank-fishing room, so it sees some bait-fishing pressure and get its share of planted trout. It may also contain some wild fish, but they'd just stocked it when I went there, so it was hard to get past the hordes of cookie-cutter planters to catch anything better. It's a shallow lake, too, surrounded by reeds in many places, so the best way to fly fish it is from a float tube. In fact, it would be a good place to make a start if you're new to float tubing.

To get there, immediately opposite the junction of Highway 89 with Highway 88 in Hope Valley, turn south in Hope Valley on an unmarked road. The road quickly becomes dirt, suitable only for high-clearance vehicles, and leads to Burnside Lake in 7 miles.

West Fork of the Carson River, Hope Valley. The slow water in the meadow offers challenging angling.

THE WEST FORK OF THE CARSON RIVER
DeLorme: p. 90, C1–B2
USFS: Toiyabe National Forest
USGS: Carson Pass, Freel Peak, Woodfords
Altitude: 8200–5400 feet
Water types: A meadow stream, then pools and pocket water.
Trout: Browns, 9–16 inches; rainbows, 8–12 inches; brook trout,
6–10 inches in the headwaters.

When you drive Highway 89 south from Lake Tahoe, you descend from Luther Pass into wide-open Hope Valley, one of three similar valleys that the early settlers named Faith, Hope, and Charity. The meanders of a small trout stream can be glimpsed, running through the lovely meadows below. It's the West Fork of the Carson River, which has roughly one-third the flow of the better-known East Fork. It also gets heavy bait-fishing pressure, since it's so easy to park next to the highway, stroll a few yards, and dunk bait from the level, grassy bank, all the while keeping an eye on the kids. This bait-fishing pressure, combined with the low, clear flows of late summer, tends to make fly fishers ignore the river. In truth, though, it holds more wild trout than the East Fork, although the fish are quite a bit smaller.

The West Fork originates as the outflow of the Lost Lakes and joins Forestdale Creek in little Faith Valley. It's a tiny stream there, bordered by low willows in a meadow heavily grazed by cattle. There's not much cover for trout, and the flow really drops to a trickle in the late summer, so the trout are all little brookies. Then the stream flows through a shallow canyon with small pools and runs that harbor a few rainbows and browns, as well as the brookies. It arrives in Hope Valley, where its flow is increased a bit by Red Lake Creek. It's a pool-and-riffle stream there, with unstable, grassy banks, though some big rocks provide cover. The few undercut banks and the pocket water occasionally can harbor surprisingly large brown trout, but stealth will be needed to catch them.

At the end of Hope Valley, opposite Sorensen's Resort, the river gathers pace, and some nice rocky runs contain wild browns. The river then drops into a steep, narrow canyon, paralleled all the way by the highway. There are four campgrounds through here and a private resort, so the fishing pressure is considerable. The surprise, though, is that while the large pools may be devoid of trout other than planters, the shallow runs and pocket water can be full of wild rainbows and browns. The rainbows are deeply colored beauties, strongly contrasting with the planters, whose gray backs are easy to spot in the water. Insect life is abundant throughout the river, with plentiful mayflies, Little Yellow and Golden Stoneflies, and some small tan caddisflies.

The river is easily accessed from Highway 88, which parallels it through much of Hope Valley and throughout the canyon. Highway 89 crosses the river just before its junction with Highway 88, then again at Woodfords, below the canyon. Faith Valley can be accessed off Blue Lakes Road, which heads south from Highway 88, 2.7 miles west of its junction with Highway 89.

RED LAKE CREEK
DeLorme: p. 90, C1
USFS: Toiyabe National Forest
USGS: Carson Pass
Altitude: 7900–7300 feet
Water types: A tiny meadow stream with some pools and runs.
Trout: Brook trout, 6–10 inches; rainbows, 7–10 inches.

Red Lake Creek can provide entertaining fishing. It's always had one of the most numerous trout populations in the Carson drainage. Indeed, the only survey Fish and Game conducted here, back in 1983, showed it had 2000 trout per mile, a lot for a tiny stream. However, a wader-clad angler couldn't wave a 9-foot rod around without feeling utterly ridiculous. It's so tiny that you can step across it in places—a jump would be overkill. But the miniature runs and pools do hide some trout capable of putting a respectable bend in a small, light rod. They just don't have anywhere to run.

You cross the creek twice on Highway 88 below Carson Pass, just after you pass its source at Red Lake. The Department of Fish and Game purchased the water rights in the lake a few years ago to improve flows in the West Walker through Hope Valley, so the flow is fairly consistent year-round. A pleasant meadow can be found downstream of the second bridge over the creek. The stream then flows under Blue Lakes Road, but it's private land above the bridge.

WILLOW CREEK
DeLorme: p. 90, B1
USFS: Toiyabe National Forest
USGS: Freel Peak
Altitude: 8600–7200 feet
Water types: A little meadow stream, then pools and runs.
Trout: Brook trout, 6–9 inches; rainbows, 7–10 inches.

Little Willow Creek is named for the silver willows that line the banks, but they don't seem to obstruct casting too much. It rises beneath Freel Peak in Horse Meadow, high above Hope Valley, then flows through a large, beautiful meadow filled with blue gentians, monkshood, and Jacob's ladder to join the West Fork of the Carson. It passes through some wooded terrain on the way, with some log structure and rocky pools, but even in the meadows, it doesn't hang about, flowing strongly through the undercuts.

Perhaps because of the consistently fast water, trout don't seem to get as big as they might, though I may simply have failed to catch the larger ones. They're rainbows in the wooded sections, little brook trout in the meadows. The creek would provide a relaxing side trip from the West Carson, when the latter turns sulky in the middle of a hot sunny day. The lower meadow, a short walk from Hope Valley, would be a lovely place for a family picnic, from which a dutiful father—or mother, of course—might escape for a cast or two.

Coming down Highway 89 from South Lake Tahoe, you'll see a gated road on your left, about half a mile before the junction with Highway 88, with a big "Road Closed" sign. Park there and walk in to a bridge over the creek, then fish up or down. You will find the large meadow less than half a mile upstream.

RED LAKE
DeLorme: p. 90, C1
USFS: Toiyabe National Forest
USGS: Carson Pass
Altitude: 7900 feet
Trout: Planted and wild brook trout, plus some cutthroats.

Red Lake is an attractive man-made lake nestling beneath the spectacular bare rock of the well-named Red Peak at Carson Pass. The banks are clothed with aspens, pines, and willows. This lake is owned and managed by the Department of Fish and Game as a trophy brook trout fishery, for which it's ideally suited because of its fertility. The fertility is demonstrated by the green algae suspended in the water and the presence of scuds. If you lift out a handful of rooted weeds, you'll see these little olive-gray crustaceans wriggling among them. Like the other man-made lakes in the area, it also contains blood midges, a hatch well worth imitating. Brook trout with some size to them are planted here, but brookies don't seem to suffer from the eroded fins that afflict hatchery rainbows, so they'll be pretty hard to tell from the wild fish, anyway.

You'll pass the lake just below Carson Pass on Highway 88. Turn right onto a paved road that leads to the dam, where you can park. There's also a dirt road before that, leading to a rocky promontory next to a shallow bay on the north shore. There is bank-fishing room, but the lake's ideally suited to float tubing. Watch out for wind in the afternoons, though. It blows straight down from the pass toward the dam, leaving little of the lake sheltered.

There are many other lakes in the vicinity. **Crater Lake** and **Scott Lake** are reached by four-wheel-drive roads off Highway 88 and contain small brook trout.

On Blue Lakes Road, which loops around just below the Sierra crest, you'll find the fairly large **Blue Lakes, Twin Lake,** and **Meadow Lake,** all planted with rainbows and cutthroats. The first 6 miles of the road are paved, while the rest is fairly well-packed dirt.

Tamarack Lake, Sunset Lakes, Summit Lake, and **Wet Meadows Reservoir** are on a spur road off Blue Lakes Road and accessible by high-clearance vehicles only. They contain cutthroats, rainbows, and/or brook trout.

Raymond Lake is about a mile's steep hike past Wet Meadows Reservoir, but it does contain golden trout.

INDIAN CREEK RESERVOIR
DeLorme: p. 90, B/C2
USFS: Toiyabe National Forest
USGS: Markleeville
Altitude: 5600 feet
Trout: Planted rainbows, brook trout, and Kamloops rainbows.

Indian Creek Reservoir is yet another highly fertile water-supply reservoir. In fact, it's so fertile that a broad band of rooted weeds and green algae stretches out from every bank for ten yards or more, so it can be fished only from a float tube, canoe, or pram. The reservoir gets drawn down in the summer, but it's still an attractive place, with high mountains towering to the north and dry hills to the south dotted with pine trees. There are two dams, separated by a rocky peninsula. The lake received Lahontan cutthroats in the past, but is currently planted with brook trout, Kamloops, and regular rainbows. The Kamloops are lovely, deep-bodied fish with an even pink blush to their sides and fewer spots than a regular rainbow. They fight hard and were running between 11 and 14 inches, though if they overwinter, they should get to 20 inches, maybe bigger. This lake has the potential to grow big fish, if they don't get taken. The brookies were planted as fingerlings in 1997, so it remains to be seen how big they'll get.

The fertile soup of algae supports a population of blood midges, varying, as usual, in size and color. Callibaetis mayflies hatch in the mornings, followed by a spinner fall, then the blood midges hatch in the evening, together with some caddisflies that will be responsible for the occasional splashy rise. The majority of the fish will be cruising, however, leaving delicate little swirls as they sip the helpless midge pupae off the underside of the surface film. Simply cast a midge emerger out to intercept them and let it sit. It's a tense, exciting way to fish.

Turn south on Highway 89 at Woodfords, then left onto Airport Road shortly before Markleeville. It's 3.5 miles to the lake, with the campground and boat ramp to the left, while a dirt road on the right leads to a rough boat launch and parking area. The campground is quite deluxe, with hot showers.

Lodging

Hope Valley

Sorensen's Resort
Charming, cozy cabins and
a restaurant
1-800-423-9949

Hope Valley Resort
Tent cabins and a rental house
1-800-423-9949

Woodfords

Woodfords Inn
A modern motel on Highway 89
(530) 694-2410

Markleeville

Alpine Inn Motel
on High Street
(530) 694-2591
J Marklee Toll Station Motel
on High Street
(530) 694-2507

East Fork Resort
Basic cabins on Highway 89
(530) 694-2229

The old Alpine Hotel in Markleeville no longer provides lodging, but it does contain the wonderfully funky Cutthroat Saloon and a pretty good restaurant.

Campsites

All are National Forest Service campgrounds unless otherwise stated. Those that charge a fee are operated by concessionaires and cost an average of $10 per site. Sites at those marked with the telephone icon ☎ can be reserved by calling 1-800-280-CAMP.

Hope Valley ☎
Blue Lakes Road
Fee, piped water

Kit Carson
Highway 88
Fee, piped water

Snowshoe Springs
Highway 88
Fee, piped water

Crystal Springs
Highway 88
Fee, piped water

Turtle Rock
County Park
Off Highway 89
Fee, piped water

Indian Creek (BLM)
At Indian Creek Reservoir
Fee, hot showers, water

Hot Springs State Park
Hot Springs Road
Fee, hot showers, water
(for reservations call 1-800-444-PARK)

Markleeville
Highway 89
Fee, piped water

Centerville Flats
Highway 4
No fee, no water

Wolf Creek
4 miles off Highway 4
No fee, no water

Silver Creek ☎
Highway 4
Fee, piped water

The Toiyabe National Forest provides plenty of rough camping spots along Blue Lakes Road, Hot Springs Road, and at the entrance to Pleasant Valley. You can get a hot shower at Grover Hot Springs State Park by paying the day-use fee.

BACKCOUNTRY PACK TRIPS

To arrange horseback trips into the Carson Iceberg Wildeness, contact The Little Antelope Pack Stations at (530) 495-2443.

SUPPLIES

A small selection of flies, leaders, and accessories is available at the Markleeville General Store, together with groceries and camping supplies. You also can get groceries and fill propane tanks at Sierra Pines, on the west side of Highway 89, north of Markleeville, or at the East Fork Resort, south of town on Highway 89. The Deli in Markleeville makes good sandwiches.

INDEX OF STREAMS AND LAKES